Learning to TRUST God

LEGACY PRESS

Learning to TRUST God

Deborah J. Kern

To Chuck, who has lived this book with me.
To Marci, who was first to encourage and support my writing.
To my parents, Walt and Jula, whose lives are an example.
And to my faithful friends and companions on the journey.

LEARNING TO TRUST GOD

ISBN 1-885358-99-7
Legacy reorder# LP46983

Legacy Press
P.O. Box 261129
San Diego, CA 92196

Printed in the United States of America

Contents

Preface

The morning air was crisp and cold. We hurried from the car to the restaurant. Giant mounds of snow, pushed to the side when the roads were cleared, created a slippery hazard to climb over as we made our way from the parking lot to the front door.

When we entered the charming little house that had been converted into a restaurant, I smiled. The smells were wonderful. "I'm glad we found this place," I said.

My husband and I had been in the Lake Tahoe area for four days on a short skiing vacation with our children, Matthew and Jula. It was our last morning, so we had decided to have a relaxing Sunday brunch before heading to San Francisco for Matt to catch his flight back to college.

The restaurant was packed. We had to wait for a table, but we were still in "vacation mode," so we didn't mind waiting. We read the newspaper and chatted about our skiing adventures until we were seated. While we were leisurely eating our breakfast, Matthew looked at his watch and said thoughtfully, "You know, my flight leaves at 4:30 and we still have a good 3-1/2 to 4-hour drive."

I looked at the time and, without really thinking about it, said, "I'm sure we'll be okay."

Matt shrugged his shoulders and said, "Oh, I'm not worried." But as we finished breakfast I began to do some mental calculations and thought, *We really do need to get going.* We finished breakfast and returned to our rented condominium to pack up before heading home.

As we started on our way, I looked at the time and thought, *We really are cutting it close.* When we got to the freeway we could see that the weekend traffic had already begun to thicken. I looked at the clock on the dash and out of the corner of my eye I saw my husband, Chuck, glance at his watch. We were both thinking the same thing. Matt's chances of making his flight didn't look good.

We talked about it for a minute and Matt said, "Well, if I don't make it, I don't make it. I'll just catch a later flight."

Matt's ticket, however, was a non-refundable economy fare. The thought of having to purchase another plane ticket was all the incentive Chuck needed — he began to drive as only he can when he's in a hurry, changing lanes and not letting the heavy traffic slow him down. I gritted my teeth and hung on! We both watched the miles and the clock, trying to figure out if we'd make it and Matt…well, Matt curled up his long frame in the back seat and slept.

Throughout the afternoon, Chuck and I kept recalculating our chances, revising estimates whenever the traffic slowed and wondering about the possibilities of getting him another flight on a busy Sunday night and how much we'd have to pay for another ticket. We watched for the highway patrol and checked the maps for possible detours through heavy traffic areas, while Matt…continued to sleep.

A couple of times I looked back at him sleeping so peacefully. "He's certainly unconcerned," I commented to Chuck. Glancing back in the rear view mirror, Chuck smiled ruefully. "Although, I guess he doesn't need to be," I continued. "That's always our department."

Why should Matt have been concerned? He knew his dad would take care of it. He would either get him there or buy him another ticket. It wasn't his responsibility, so why worry?

During the last hour, he awakened and asked us to turn on the radio. Relaxed and happy, he did some homework, then leaned forward to chat about some of his classes.

Chuck continued to push on. We finally blew into the airport with only minutes to spare. With a quick hug, Matt grabbed his bag and ran for the plane. Turning to smile and wave, he disappeared into the airport. Exhausted, Chuck and I got back into the car and made our way home.

We both smiled again as we discussed Matt's lack of concern as we sweated out every mile trying to get him to the airport in time. It must be nice to be that carefree, we remarked, to be able to just put yourself in another's care.

As I thought about our ride home from the mountains I thought, *Wouldn't it be great if life could be like that? Wouldn't it be wonderful to be so confident of our care that we could just rest and enjoy the ride?*

As Christians, that's how our lives should be. But they usually aren't. The journey through life doesn't resemble Matt's trip at all. Instead, it's filled with uncertainty and fear as we frantically scan the horizon ahead and wonder what will happen, or look out the windows beside us and allow our immediate surroundings to destroy our joy and peace. We stare at the road behind, questioning, "Why did we come this way?"

The Word of God says, "You will keep him in perfect peace, whose mind is stayed on you, because he trusts in you." Isaiah 26:3 (NKJV).

A peaceful journey through life? That isn't what life is like for most of us. Why is there so much anxiety and fear? Why is there so much confusion?

The answer is in the last part of the verse with its explanation of how someone lives in peace: "...because he trusts in you."

Matt had learned he could trust his father. After all, his dad had taken care of him for 19 years. He was completely confident in his ability to continue to do so.

If we don't live in peace, rest and security, it's because we haven't yet learned to trust in our heavenly Father. We're uncertain of His ability to take care of us and unsure of His desire to do so.

God wants us to be able to trust Him. All of His interactions with people — from the first separation in the garden and throughout history — have focused on drawing people back into the kind of relationship they were created to enjoy with Him: loving and intimate and based on trust — trust in God's goodness and trust in His desire to always do good for us.

Sin made it difficult to trust God, not because God changed, but because we did. Sin changed us and it changed the world. It brought evil, pain and a separation that obscures the face of God for us. We see the evil, we experience the pain and sorrow, and we find it hard to see and know God.

That lack of knowledge about God and His character means we have difficulty knowing Him as trustworthy, but our heavenly Father wants us to know we are always safe with Him and to learn that we can trust Him. He wants us to be able to travel through life without allowing our emotions to be in a perpetual state of turmoil. We do not need to always sit on the edge in fear.

He knows that trusting Him in the middle of a hurting, sin-cursed world will not be easy. Sometimes it will seem easier for us to give in to the pain and bewilderment than to look to Him in trust. He knows it is sometimes easier to wallow in our anxiety and misery, and our self-pity and blame, than to turn to Him in love and acceptance of all that comes our way.

And He knows it will sometimes be easier for us to settle into a permanent attitude of distance with Him when we've been hurt and confused by life's tough situations.

So God lovingly begins to coax us. He takes control of situations, helps us through problems and brings His good into our lives over and over again. Slowly, He begins to teach us that we can trust Him.

It is important to realize that you'll never be happy as a Christian until you learn to trust God. External circumstances will rule your life and your emotions. You'll never get past your own childish perception of things and you'll always hold back from submitting to God in all. The path you walk will be formed by outside circumstances and littered with the problems you will create.

God's desire for our lives is that we have a secure and trusting relationship with Him. Accepting Christ as Savior is only the first step. From that point on, we gradually learn to trust in God. Each step progresses us further along. It's a process, and the steps involved are sometimes difficult, and sometimes long and labored, but always guided by our heavenly Father. This process is described best in Proverbs 3:5-6.

"Trust in the Lord with all your heart…"

In learning to trust God we must decide what we believe about God and His involvement in our lives. In order to lay a foundation for trust, we must grasp God's sovereignty and decide that no matter what happens we WILL trust God.

"…and lean not on your own understanding…"

We have to learn that our understanding only brings fear and turmoil. We have to become willing to let go of our limited perspectives and accept the faith and understanding that He gives.

"…in all your ways acknowledge Him…"

We also have to learn that fully trusting God means full submission to Him in every part of our lives. We must be willing to "acknowledge" Him in the circumstances that come our way, knowing if He allowed it, He wants to bring good from it. We'll come to realize that He is interested in all of life — from the momentous to the mundane.

"...and He shall direct your path." Proverbs 3:5-6

As we let go of our own understanding and submit our lives to Him, God directs our ways in order to put us on His perfect path and bring good from every circumstance. As we move toward trust in God, the truths in Proverbs 3:5-6 begin to work together, creating a spiral effect as each reinforces and enhances the others.

* * *

For me, learning to trust God has been an intense, exciting, life-changing and sometimes wrenching spiritual journey. My experience hasn't been one born from tragedy, but out of the need to know God was there in the everyday ups and downs, the times of tremendous stress and the days of dark uncertainty — in all the circumstances of my life.

Out of this desire (and, at times, the desperate need) to know God was there, has come the gradual awareness that God Himself wants me to know and trust Him and has been faithfully working toward that end. Pushing, pulling, prodding and shoving me into new awareness, new surrender and new faith, He has coaxed me over and over to trust in Him. He has used His best tools — my circumstances — to maneuver me toward confrontation, change, understanding, obedience and trust.

The purpose of this book is not to engage in a theological debate regarding the role of God in the circumstances of people. It is also not an attempt to bring solace to the person in the middle of tragedy, although I believe implicit trust does bring comfort. Rather, my intent is to give a practical outline to God's work in us during the ups and downs of life: to bring peace where there is anxiety, rest where there is turmoil and trust where there is unbelief and fear.

God does not waste anything! He wants to use every part of our lives to teach us more about Him, to draw us to seek Him and respond to Him and to enable us to learn to trust Him.

The Lord gives strength to His people; the Lord blesses His people with peace.

— Psalm 29:11

Part One

Trust in the Lord with All Your Heart

Can God Be Trusted?

For me, learning to trust God started in a small way.

I only worked one day a week at my husband's office, but my children were young and leaving them with a sitter always made me feel guilty. In order to alleviate those feelings, I would often take them to get doughnuts on the way to the sitter's home. This was a treat, so it made them happy and I didn't feel so bad about leaving them. Of course, I felt guilty about feeding them such junk for breakfast, but guilt seems to be an inescapable fact of motherhood.

One morning, after getting doughnuts and dropping off the kids at the sitter's, I entered the freeway for the 40-minute drive to work. I enjoyed those moments by myself and usually used the time to think and pray.

That particular morning, I was about halfway to work when I reached into my purse for my lipstick (the final touches of grooming were sometimes overlooked in the rush to get two toddlers and myself out the door that early!).

As my hand felt its way around my compact, notebook, pens, crackers and tissue to grasp the lipstick, I noticed my purse felt odd. I looked down and realized my wallet was missing. I searched through the car as I kept an eye on the freeway, but the wallet was not there.

I tried to remember where I had left it, as pictures of credit cards, checks, ID and money flashed before my eyes.

Trying to fight the depression as anxiety increased, I asked for God's help. Instantly, His peace enveloped me. I felt Him say, "Don't worry, I've taken care of it."

I began to rejoice in His words and presence, but my rational mind began to question, "God, is this really you? Are you really concerned with something like this?"

I was able to pray about the loss but not willing to believe in His concern.

God's unmistakable presence stilled my questioning heart. In the stillness, He again spoke to my spirit. "I've taken care of it! Losing your wallet, and the hassle that would bring, is not in my plan for you today. If I can't bring good out of something, no matter how small, I won't allow it into your life. I will never let anything touch you from which I can't bring good."

I marveled at the words, thanking God for His goodness and care, but then in the next minute questioned, "Really, God? Is this You? This is just a wallet we're talking about here. You care about that?"

I continued to think about what I felt He was saying, remembering the familiar text in Romans 8:28: "We know that in all things God works for the good of those who love Him." The words spoken into my mind certainly seemed to line up with that Scripture, but was it really as simple as that?

When I got to work, a man had already called and left a message for me. Apparently I had laid the wallet on top of the car at the donut shop while I buckled the kids into their car seats, then forgot about it as I hopped into the car and drove off. The wallet stayed there until I reached the middle of the busy six-lane street next to the donut shop.

It must have been there for only a moment before a man on his way to work spotted it in the road and stopped to pick it up. Upon arriving at his office he found my husband's business card in the wallet and called. No problems, no hassles; I was able to drive by his office on my way home that afternoon and pick it up.

Minor incident? Yes. Coincidence? Some would say so. But God planted a seed of truth that morning that He has continued to grow and deepen over the years: He is interested in every part of my life. Whenever I begin to doubt His part in the small details, the life-changing events or the hard circumstances that touch my life, He patiently reminds me of the truth He impressed upon me that day over 20 years ago, the truth that is in His word:

God, <u>who is the blessed controller of all things</u>, the King over all kings and the master of all masters, the only source of immortality.

— 1 Timothy 6:15 (PHILLIPS)

* * *

Learning to trust God — believing that He brings good from everything that touches my life — has not always been as easy as the lesson learned the day I lost my wallet. I've faced much more wrenching circumstances in which I did not see God's intervention. I've wrestled with many questions, and the answers didn't come overnight.

I still had to struggle with the concept of God's trustworthiness when it was placed next to the reality of the world in which I lived and the circumstances of life that stared me in the face. There was a lot happening in the world and in my life from which it seemed He couldn't possibly bring "good," and a lot of questions about His role in it all.

Perhaps as you are reading this, your insides are knotting and your thoughts are automatically going to the tragedy that has happened to you or the difficult circumstances you face right now. You are thinking, *How can I believe God is "the blessed controller of all things" when He allowed ____________________ to happen?*

A few years ago I sat talking to two beautiful young women who were staying in our home for a few days. They were sisters who had lost their mother to cancer just months before. As we discussed the grief process and the difficulties in finding God's role in this tragedy, one of them said, "I decided very soon after her death that God was not a part of it. It was the only way I could deal with it and still retain a close relationship with God."

"But now that choice, that belief, has left me grappling with other issues. If He wasn't a part of that, then what is He part of?"

What we believe about God's role in people's circumstances can become an all-consuming question as we struggle to make sense of the circumstances in which we find ourselves, whether they are life-altering, horrible situations or the more normal upheavals and disappointments of life. And the beliefs we have about God's role in the circumstances of the world will become much more important and our questioning more desperate when we find ourselves in painful circumstances. Our intellectual reasoning and conclusions may become powerless to help us as we grapple with the emotions of bewilderment, hurt and anger.

The journey to trust and to understand God's ways didn't happen overnight for me and it won't for you. However, the first step is dealing with the questions. Is He "the blessed controller of all things"? Can He care for us, even in a world that is in disarray?

Can God Be Trusted?

We want to think so. But sometimes the cruel facts of the world in which we live are more apparent to us than God's trustworthiness is.

We'd like to trust Him and feel secure in His love and care, but can we? Often our trust is hindered by a philosophy about God that we've developed to make ourselves feel better during difficult days, and the answers we've chosen to our questions regarding God's hand in our lives.

A friend of mine once said, "I trust God. It's other people I don't trust."

I listened to an associate pastor tell a young married class one day, "Don't bother God with your trivial problems. He isn't interested."

Someone was talking last week about a tough situation that he was facing, and he ended by saying, "Well, that's life!" He was right. That is life, but how do we as Christians fit "life" with belief in God? Can we do that and still trust in Him?

There are writings and philosophies that run the gamut from "God isn't involved in our personal lives at all" to "God causes and sends everything that comes our way, good and bad." Then there is the classic explanation for the evil that surrounds us: "God can't intervene in the world because of man's free will, so you and I just have to put up with the evil."

We then are left with the struggles of our own personal beliefs. Do we believe God intervenes and is concerned with daily life? Is He interested in each of us personally? Will He intervene? How can I trust Him if He doesn't? Does He really notice and care about what goes on in the world? Or, does He just let the world go on in its own momentum with the sinfulness that causes evil and pain?

Does our free will mean He can't intervene? How else can we explain the tragedies? Is His purpose to simply save us and prepare us for the eternal relationship we will have with Him? Are we "on our own" here on earth?

Is He "the blessed controller of all things"?

God's Word says to trust Him:

The Lord's unfailing love surrounds the man who trusts in Him.

–Psalm 32:10

Do not let your hearts be troubled. Trust in God: trust also in me.

–John 14:1

But can we? So many questions hinder our ability to trust in God with all our heart!

At whatever point you are in your journey to trusting God, what you believe about God and His role in the circumstances of life will have everything to do with your subsequent journey of faith.

The Blessed Controller

The phrase that I've used over and over again, "God, who is the blessed controller of all things," may or may not be a comfort to you at this time. Whatever your response, depending on your circumstances, memorize the phrase and allow it to be a part of your thought life.

You may have always believed "all things work together for good" and other Scriptures that help us to trust, but at this moment the pain of your circumstances is overwhelming any past knowledge of God's goodness. You may be struggling with unanswered questions, anger and bitterness. Give God an opening by saying, "God, I want to trust You and feel close again, but I just can't. Please help me." Allow God to bring peace and healing back into your wounded soul.

Study

What do the following Scriptures say about God?

Nehemiah 9:6 ______________________________

Psalm 33:13-15 ______________________________

Psalm 47:7 ______________________________

Psalm 75:2-3 ______________________________

Psalm 139:7-10 ______________________________

Jeremiah 23:23-24 ______________________________

Look up Psalm 25 and say the first two lines out loud as a prayer. Make yourself say it even if the feelings are not there yet. Begin to pray daily, "Lord, enable me to trust you."

Memorize

God…who is the blessed controller of all things. 1 Timothy 6:15 (PHILLIPS)

Prayer of Response

Dear God, I want to believe that You are in control of everything that happens to me. It's difficult to reconcile all of the pain and suffering with your goodness, but I ask for help in believing You are sovereign and good! Help me to believe that You will bring good from everything that touches my life. Amen.

Reflect

1. Are you aware that God sees and considers everything you do?
2. Do you really believe it?
3. How does that make you feel?
4. What is the biggest obstacle to your trust in God?

Can God Care for Me in a World Full of Evil?

Daily, we are bombarded with headlines blaring tragedies: murders, starving multitudes, abused children. How can God take care of us in a world filled with the sorrow and pain that He allows to continue?

How can we explain God's role in these circumstances? In order to deal with the reality of evil and still believe in the goodness of God, some choose to believe that God cannot stop evil because of the limits He has imposed upon Himself to give people free will.

This gets God "off the hook" in one sense. The young woman who lost her mother used this philosophy in order to deal with her mother's death. Unfortunately, as she was finding, when we take God out of one circumstance we have to take Him out of others as well. What is He part of? And if we carry out this philosophy to its logical conclusion, it also renders Him powerless on our behalf, and how then can we trust Him? Can we trust a God who has made Himself impotent in the face of evil?

Can we trust God if we're not sure He can or will prevent the tragedies that may lie in our paths?

I've already mentioned 1 Timothy 6:15, which describes God as "the blessed and only Ruler," or as J. B. Phillips (1958) translates it: "God…who is the blessed controller of all things."

Psalm 22:28 tells us "dominion belongs to the Lord and he rules over the nations."

These Scriptures, along with others that are similar, must undergird what we know and believe about God. Everything else must come into alignment with it.

God's Word says that He is sovereign over the world and all in it. But what about free will? How does that fit in? God's Word does say that people are free to choose their destiny: "If anyone chooses to do God's will." (John 7:17)

God is sovereign and people are free. Do these two facts contradict one another? Does one negate the other? Does our free will mean that God can't intervene in the events of life, in the circumstances that are so often caused by the choices sinful people make? If God, as sovereign, intervenes in the world, has He crossed over His decision to create people as free agents?

God's Word also says that we can trust Him. But how can we if our free will means God cannot intervene?

If God, who is sovereign, omniscient and unchanging, has created people and given them free choice, then God, as Creator, is the standard by which all truth must be measured.

His sovereignty and our free will are fact, but there is nothing in the Word of God that says God has to make Himself impotent in order to give us a choice. He has not laid down His power and control over the world in order to give us free will. He does not have to!

He has, however, allowed the world to suffer the consequences of their choices and sinfulness. Every Scripture that talks of our choices also speaks of the results of those decisions — blessings for those who choose to obey and trust God, cursing for those who do not.

See, I am setting before you today a blessing and a curse — the blessing if you obey the commands of the Lord your God that I am giving you today; the curse if you disobey the commands of the Lord your God and turn from the way that I command you.

–Deuteronomy 11:26-28

People make choices day in and day out, moment by moment. Those choices, good and bad, create the circumstances of the world in which we live. What power seems to lie within each of us! But are these daily choices guaranteed us by God's gift of free will?

* * *

Richard's life, like yours and mine, was full of choices. But Richard, because of his higher-than-average intelligence, his athletic talents and his handsome appearance, probably had more options than many. His abilities in high school sports gave him the opportunity to choose from a number of colleges. His grades and class standing in college meant he had more career opportunities than most others.

Richard <u>chose</u> a college. He <u>chose</u> a wife during his senior year, and he <u>chose</u> a company to work for in the part of the country where he wanted to live.

As he and his wife started their life together, they <u>chose</u> to work and buy a home before starting a family. They <u>chose</u> to buy a cabin in the mountains and to spend some time traveling. They <u>chose</u> to use their free time pursuing their many hobbies and interests. What a wonderful life they "created" with their <u>choices.</u>

Then one day as Richard sat at his desk, in the chosen company of his well-chosen life, a deranged former employee with a grudge to settle burst into the office and killed seven people who happened to be in his way. Richard was one of them.

This man made a choice that snuffed out lives within the space of a heartbeat. All of Richard's choices were gone. Were the other man's choices more powerful than Richard's? Who decides? Destiny? Chance? God?

It is ironic that with all of our options and all of our abilities to "choose" what we do with our lives, we have no guarantee of life and no guarantee of the power of our free will to "create" choices. The only undeniable* choice we will ever have is freedom to choose whether or not we will accept or reject God. This is the "free will" that you and I are given as God-created beings — the ability to choose whether or not we will have a relationship with God.

Whenever God's Word mentions our choices, it is always our choice to choose or reject God and His commands: "Choose for yourselves this day whom you will serve." Joshua 24:15

Our free will does extend to our daily lives. God does allow people to pursue their own paths, usually without apparent intervention in their decisions. However, He has already ordained the consequences of our choices: blessing or cursing (see Leviticus, chapter 23). Sin and suffering are the results of a world that rejects God.

For those who choose God and a relationship with Him, God's sovereignty becomes their security, their basis for trust. And God is sovereign.

Yours, O Lord, is the greatness and the power, and the glory and the majesty and the splendor, for everything in heaven and earth is yours. Yours, O Lord, is the kingdom; you are exalted as head over all. Wealth and honor come from you; you are the ruler of all things.

–1 Chronicles 29:11-12

Not only is God sovereign, but His Word says in Ephesians 1:13 that His people are set apart. Proverbs 2:7-8 says, "[The Lord] is a shield to those whose walk is blameless, for he guards the course of the just and protects the way of his faithful ones."

Our sovereign God can and will intervene in people's lives to accomplish His purposes and protect His children. As we put our lives into His hands, His care and control will become more and more evident.

2 Peter 2:4-9 reminds us of Old Testament events: God rescued Lot while still bringing judgment upon Sodom and Gomorrah. He saved Noah while He destroyed an evil world. Peter goes on to say, "If this is so, then the Lord knows how to rescue godly men from trials."

Our free will is not destroyed when God intervenes to accomplish His purposes. God will never change a person's will to choose or not choose Him*, and God does not usually interfere in our decisions. He simply allows us to suffer the consequences of our own sinful natures. However, He can and does block a person's direction or intent if it does not coincide with His perfect will.

A creative God like ours is not without recourse even when our free will is operating. God hardened Pharaoh's heart in order to accomplish His purpose for the children of Israel. Was He taking away Pharaoh's free will? No, Pharaoh's will was set against God already. God saw a will that was set against His sovereignty. He hardened Pharaoh's heart against the Israelites so that His omnipotence and power to deliver could be shown.

God can turn the evil intents of people away from us, if He chooses. "The king's heart is in the hand of the Lord; he directs it like a watercourse wherever he pleases." Proverbs 21:1

The Bible is full of stories of God's intervention in people's lives, and He will still step in to protect the lives of His children.

He has asked us to trust Him because He is trustworthy.

The Lord watches over you…
The Lord will keep you from all harm —
he will watch over your life.

– Psalm 121:5-7

Accepting God's Sovereignty

This chapter's purpose is to give you a foundation in God's sovereignty, based on a logical interpretation of Scripture within the context of free will. If you have further questions about these concepts, turn to page 285 for a list of recommended readings that will provide you with a more in-depth study. It is vital that you grasp the truth of God's sovereignty! Your well-being and your walk with God hinge upon it. You can never be truly intimate with a God you can't depend upon or trust.

God wants you to know His sovereignty. Knowing God begins with believing what the Word of God says about Him. You will never have the joy and peace God intends for you without this "foundation of belief."

If you are reading this in the middle of a painful time, the fact of God's sovereignty may not be a comfort to you right now. Again, I encourage you to plunge ahead with any submission and trust you can muster. Pray, "Lord, the thought of Your sovereignty in light of what has happened [or what is happening] to me is not a source of comfort right now. I ask You to help me to find my way back to trust in You."

Study

What do James 4:13-15, Proverbs 16:9 and Lamentations 3:37 say about our plans? ______________________________

According to the following Scriptures, what is under God's control?

Job 14:5 ______________________________

Psalm 22:28 ______________________________

Psalm 139:13-16 ______________________________

Psalm 148:8 ______________________________

Isaiah 14:26-27; 46:10-11 ______________________________

Daniel 5:21 ______________________________

Acts 17:24-28 ______________________________

Ephesians 1:20-21 ______________________________

Read the story of Nebuchadnezzar in Daniel, chapter 4. Underline verses 17b, 25b, 26b, 34 and 35. What did God want Nebuchadnezzar to know? ______________________________

____

____

Memorize

How great are his signs! and how mighty are his wonders! His kingdom is an everlasting kingdom, and his dominion is from generation to generation. Daniel 4:3

Prayer of Response

Dear Father, I want to be able to trust You. Please begin to build in me a foundation of belief; belief in Your sovereignty over all things and belief in Your ability to bring good from all circumstances. I want the knowledge of Your sovereign power over the world in which I live to begin to permeate my life, making a difference in my attitude toward the circumstances of my life. Amen.

Reflect

1. What do you believe about God's role in the world?
2. What is the basis for your belief?

*I realize the extent of people's free will is a matter that has been debated for centuries as scholars have grappled with what seems to many the paradox of God's sovereignty and people's free will. For a look at several interpretations, I recommend *Predestination and Free Will,* edited by David Basinger and Randall Basinger, Intervarsity Press, 1986.

Does His Care Mean I Won't Suffer?

Roger and Susan accepted Christ as teenagers. They met and married while in college, and at that time both renewed their commitments to serve God. They centered their lives and family around God and their church, faithfully giving of their time, energy and money.

With three children, a good marriage and a growing and prosperous business, they seemed to be a perfect example of God's blessing upon His obedient children.

Not long after Roger and Susan celebrated their 15th wedding anniversary, however, a new product hit the market that competed heavily with Roger's business. They didn't worry too much about it at first. God had always blessed them, and they could trust God, couldn't they?

But soon they were struggling to hang on, praying for a miracle and trying to find a way to save their business. They continued to lose customers and employees, and slowly used up their savings until the day came when they had to file bankruptcy.

Trusting God was suddenly not so easy. Roger and Susan never thought their business problems would progress that far. They were sure that God would come through with a miracle for them because they had always put Him first in their lives. But bankruptcy, losing their home and having to start all over was a bitter pill they were forced to swallow.

"Why, God?" they questioned. "Why us? Haven't we been faithful? Doesn't Your Word promise that You are faithful; that we can trust You? How could You let this happen?" They questioned God while the pressures from their circumstances forced both Roger and Susan to confront the painful fact that serving God didn't guarantee a happy outcome to all their problems.

* * *

Deciding that we can trust God seems plausible for those who have experienced relatively easy circumstances. But for those who are in the middle of events so tumultuous that their very belief in God and His goodness is threatened, it is much more difficult.

Can we accept that God allowed tragedy into our lives? Sorrow and pain will touch us, even those who accept Christ and follow God. How can we deal with that and trust Him at the same time? We can say that God did not cause the evil, but if He didn't prevent it, hasn't He failed to take care of us?

Can we accept that He knew what would happen and made the decision to remove His protection from us and allow hurtful circumstances into our lives?

As Christians, we can see over and over that God does intervene in people's lives. He changes circumstances, prevents disasters and heals sicknesses. The Bible is full of stories that tell of God's intervention. There is nothing in the Bible that implies His involvement would end after it was written.

The stories of deliverance thrill us, but the situations where divine intervention does not seem to come often leave us bewildered. What about the person who did not have his or her circumstances changed? The car didn't swerve miraculously at the last minute. The firemen didn't get there in time to save the house. The loan to save the company didn't come through. The person lying in the hospital bed, or burying a beloved child, or dealing with shattered dreams is left to ask, "Why, God?"

God's Word says that we can trust Him to care for us, but it does not say that we won't experience heartache, pain or trouble. For every Scripture we find that speaks of God's care, we can also find one that advises of "tribulation" as well.

"Isn't that a little contradictory?" we ask. "How am I to trust God?"

Psalm 91 is a thrilling reminder of God's watchful care for us, telling us that moment by moment, God is guarding and protecting us. However, look at verse 15: "I will be with him in trouble, I will deliver him."

God's provision and care is not just for protection from trouble, but in trouble — right in the middle of it.

Learning to trust God means understanding that He allows suffering into our lives, that He doesn't always intervene. It also means that we have to accept all circumstances and allow God to use them for our ultimate good. It means trusting that He knows better than we what is best for our lives and what will bring about the greatest good.

* * *

In his book *He Speaks Softly,* the late Bob Benson described retreat prayer times in which he asked people to envision a blank sheet of paper with a horizontal line across the middle. Then he asked them to recall the good things that had happened to them over the years and to "write" those one by one on the paper above the line.

Next he asked them to recall the evil things that came to them as well — the dark, troublesome times — and to list those below the line. He then reminded the participants that the whole sheet could be committed to God; that He is the God of the top list *and* the bottom list.

After this exercise, Benson said one or sometimes several people would find him to talk. The conversation was always the same:

"You know when we were listing those things on paper…and we put that stuff above and below the line? There were some things that, for the life of me, I didn't know where to put. Even now I am not sure. Some of those things are so evil it would seem their place would be a foregone conclusion. The day they happened I knew, all right. The bottom of the bottom wasn't low enough. I did not know whether I would make it or not. I thought I was going to die. But now, looking back, I'm not so sure. Some of them seem to be creeping over the line."

Then they would say, "I guess I have to write it all above the line."

* * *

Right now, you may be too close to a painful circumstance to even consider there could be "good" in it, but eventually it can become part of your personal learning-to-trust-God experience if you are willing to let God use it in your life.

We can trust God with our lives. He will not allow anything to touch us from which He cannot bring good. His Word is full of precious promises of His love and care for us, and also of His desire that we will trust Him with our lives, no matter what.

Who among all these does not know that the hand of the Lord has done this, in whose hand is the life of every living thing, and the breath of all mankind?

–Job 12:9-10 (NKJV)

* * *

"As I drove down the street where my son-in-law was staying, I was surprised to see police cars, reporters and people milling around behind a police barricade. I quickly pulled my car over and ran up to the nearest policeman to ask what was wrong."

Listening to Becky share her testimony at a women's dinner at our church, I wondered what the people around me thought. I already knew the story: the policeman pulling her aside after establishing her identity, his telling her that her daughter and four-year-old granddaughter had been beaten to death by the daughter's estranged husband, and the aftermath of coping not only with that tragedy but others. I looked around at the ladies listening so intently. Most of us would never have to deal with that kind of horror. But the questions that arise are ones we all struggle with: How can we trust a God who allows this? This woman and her daughter were Christians.

Does it help to say that God did not plan this kind of death for this young woman and her child? He would never initiate that kind of evil. The circumstances were directly attributable to sin in the world and the evil purposes of Satan, who brings turmoil, suffering and pain. Yet can we trust a God who didn't cause but "allowed" something this evil to happen?

For some reason, God chose not to stop this evil. Will we rage at God and say, "Why did You let this happen?" Our human perspective says, "God, this is unbearable and never should have happened!" In a perfect "Garden of Eden" world populated with people submitted to God, it wouldn't have. But we are no longer in the Garden and our choices continue to deny us that kind of world, so we cry, "God, why?"

We will never have all the answers to the tragedies of life. But in seeking them, especially in situations like this, we must come to God for His perspective, His insight, His comfort and, yes, His good.

God did not plan that horrible death for His two children, but He chose to allow the consequences of sin to flow unhindered that day. He did not stand in its path to stop its destructive force. Instead, He walked the path with two of His children and allowed it to continue, suffering with them in those moments. Then He transformed the destructive power into His creative good, just as He did 2,000 years ago when He allowed His own Son to be beaten and nailed to a cross.

Satan's apparent victory did not diminish God's glory. It didn't immobilize His will or thwart God's ultimate plan for His children. It never has. It never will. He chose to bring two of His children home to Him that day. Although we will have to leave in His hands the reasons why their deaths happened that way, we can remember that His Word says, "Precious in the sight of the Lord is the death of his saints." (Psalm 116:15)

Soon after their deaths, God revealed to Becky the scene in heaven when her daughter died. As she entered and saw Jesus, she immediately began to run to greet Him. He was already running to meet her.

"Oh, I'm so happy to be here!" she cried, as Jesus' arms closed around her.

Jesus laughed and, looking at her with delight, said, "I'm so glad you're here! I couldn't wait to see you." Then they turned to greet her little girl as she entered heaven's gates.

Seeing from God's perspective won't completely dissolve the pain of those who lose loved ones or those who suffer physical tragedies. Our lives will always hold trials and problems. Some seem called upon to bear tremendous suffering, but God knows from His perspective that in eternity there will be no remembrance of the pain, only joy at being with Him. We will keep the lessons learned and the victories won forever, but the pain we suffer either physically or mentally will be wiped away. The knowledge and wisdom we gain will give us the ability to know God and to have a closer and deeper relationship with Him through eternity.

As we listened to the closing words of Becky's testimony, she described the intense closeness with God that came as she agonized, as only a mother could, over a daughter dying so tragically. She explained that God drew her close and comforted her: "I know how it feels," He told her. "I watched as My Son was beaten." In those moments of solace, Becky began to feel God's anguish and His understanding of pain.

As God shared Himself with her, she knew Him as never before. Her relationship with Him deepened and grew. Yes, Becky did have to walk with God through deep shadows, but in the darkness of her circumstances, God Himself was illuminated.

Even in darkness light dawns for the upright.

–Psalm 112:4

Healing Wounds

Try Bob Benson's technique of looking back over your life. Think about where you would put some of the painful events: above the line or below?

The old adage says "time heals all wounds." That isn't necessarily true. Some wounds need to be treated before they can heal. Is there a circumstance in your past that still brings pain or bitterness toward God?

Share with God your hurt and ask Him to begin to "treat the wound." The wound may need to be reopened and looked at honestly so it can heal properly. There may be a need for forgiveness, whether it's forgiving someone else or asking for forgiveness. You may need to "forgive" God.

Study

Read Job 12:9-10, Ecclesiastes 7:14 and Lamentations 3:38. What is the central theme of these verses? ______________________________

____

____

What promises are given in Psalm 27:5 and John 16:33?

____

____

Read Genesis 1:1-10. How does verse 2 describe the earth?

____

____

What did God do with the darkness and water? What did He say about His work in verse 10? _______________________________

____

____

During Creation, God brought the darkness and deep waters under His control and used it to serve His benevolent purposes. Do you believe that God can do the same with your darkness?

____

____

Memorize

The Lord will rescue me from every evil attack and will bring me safely to his heavenly kingdom. To him be glory for ever and ever. Amen.
2 Timothy 4:18

Prayer of Response

Dear Father, You know about the pain in my heart, the feelings of regret, the feelings of betrayal, the hurt and pain that seem unending. I don't know what to do with it, how to resolve it or how to go on. I ask for Your help today. Begin the healing today and help me not to shy away from the process. Help me to take Your hand and walk forward with You into healing, restoration and, most of all, trust in You. Amen.

Reflect

1. We will examine more closely how to look at life from God's perspective later in this book, but perhaps you can already look back at an incident in your life and see it differently. What happened to change your perspective?
2. Exchanging our understanding for God's understanding means allowing His perspective to begin to balance out and eventually dominate our perceptions of events. Think about Becky's story. As we look at death from God's viewpoint, and at time from His eternal view, how could our perspectives change?

What About Other People's Choices?

"My daughter left home and is living with her boyfriend. I know they're on drugs."

"My business partner turned out to be a crook. He ran up staggering debts and then skipped out. How could he do it? I thought he was a friend."

"My husband said he just didn't want to be married anymore..."

Lives hurt by someone else. The stories are all around us. People cause us problems! They mess up our lives. They bring us pain and turmoil, and many times we feel we are at the mercy of others: the young mother whose husband leaves her with small children; the pastor who gives his life to a church only to be pushed out; the executive who is passed over for promotion not because of her lack of ability but because of company politics. Over and over we can point at situations and say, "How can we trust God when He doesn't control other's free will?"

We've already established that people have the freedom to choose their own paths, although the only guaranteed choice we have is the ability to decide whether or not we will choose God.

For those rejecting God, most of their decisions will be based on what is good for them or what they want. Their choice to deny God will cause a whole range of repercussions. The consequences filter down into many other areas — other people are always affected.

If we believe we are under God's protection and nothing touches us unless He allows it and can bring good from it, what about the circumstances that come our way through the hands of others? What about the free will of sinful people that brings its painful sting into our lives?

When we are in grievous circumstances caused by someone else, it is difficult to accept God's hand in it. "God didn't cause this. He did, or they did, or she did. God isn't a part of this!" we say, pointing a finger and succumbing to bitterness and anger.

Yet in this, too, we must learn to trust God, for "nothing that originates in the sin of man can be said to be the will of God — but by the time it reaches us, it has become God's will for us." Hannah Whitall Smith's classic explanation of God's ways in *The Christian's Secret of a Happy Life* reveals an important truth to us. We serve a creative and omniscient God who knows how to work everything for our good — so much so, that as we look back upon circumstances we have submitted to Him for His good, we can say, "God must have planned this."

Joseph is a perfect example of suffering unfairly at the hands of others. His own brothers threw him into a pit and planned his death. Instead, they sold him to passing slave traders. Joseph went from favored son to slave in a foreign country. He then rose to a place of authority in Potiphar's household, only to be abruptly thrown into prison when Potiphar's wife falsely accused him. While in prison, Joseph befriended a young man and was promised help in receiving a pardon, only to be forgotten when that young man was freed. Joseph was left to languish in prison for two more years.

If anyone had a right to succumb to bitterness over his treatment at the hands of others, Joseph did. He was a perfect candidate for distrust of God. Yet when he revealed himself to his brothers 20 years after they sold him into slavery, he said to them, "Do not be distressed and do not be angry with yourselves for selling me here, because it was to save lives that God sent me ahead of you." (Genesis 45:5)

Joseph recognized God's sovereignty in his life and learned to accept God's hand in the things that happened to him, even those things that came his way because of the actions of others.

So I reflected on all this and concluded that the righteous and the wise and what they do are in God's hands.

–Ecclesiastes 9:1

Oh, it is definitely hard to think of any good that can come when we are struggling with painful emotions, hurting and angry at people who have wronged us! Maybe as you are reading this, your insides are knotting up and your fist is unconsciously clenching. Perhaps you know personally the pain of unfair treatment. Reading a nice Bible story about Joseph isn't going to come close to making it all better for you.

This anger and bitterness has kept you from even wanting God to bring good from it. Somehow, that seems like giving in. Yet, at some point you are going to have to make the choice to let go of the bitterness and blame and accept God's role in your circumstances. Healing for you may begin when you accept that God did allow it into your life and He does want to use it for good. No matter how bad it seems, God can redeem it. But He can only do that when you turn to Him in acquiescence to His sovereignty in your life.

Jesus' death on the cross proved, and continues to prove, that God does redeem our pain and suffering. It is not without purpose. Good, beauty, grace and even joy flow out of the suffering that has been submitted to and accepted in trust.

Can you believe that behind every heartache and every sorrow is a God so wonderful, with a love so big, that knowledge of Him and intimacy with Him can obliterate every hurt? His healing touch will bring a balm to the wounds of your heart until the memory is no longer one of pain but of acceptance, peace and trust in God's ability to bring good into your life.

In God, whose word I praise,
In God I trust; I will not be afraid.
What can mortal man do to me?

–Psalm 56:4

Releasing Bitterness

Think about the hurtful circumstances that have come your way because of someone else's actions. That painful circumstance or unfair treatment was allowed by God because He saw ahead to the redemption of your suffering and the good He could bring from it. Don't thwart His desire to bring good into your life by continuing in a path of bitterness.

Even though it seems impossible to think of any good that could possibly come from your circumstance, it is time to turn your heart to God. As you seek His face and ask for His grace and help, He will extend His ability to forgive and to release the angry emotions.

Study

What do the following Scriptures say about our actions and God?

Proverbs 19:21 ______________________________

Proverbs 21:30 ______________________________

Job 12:9 ______________________________

Psalm 33:10______________________________

What was Joseph's response to his brother in Genesis 45:5?

____

____

What does Psalm 139:15-16 say about the events of your life?

____

____

Memorize

Many are the plans in a man's heart, but it is the Lord's purpose that prevails. Proverbs 19:21

Prayer of Reflection

Dear heavenly Father, I ask for Your help today. I want to lay down the resentment and anger I feel over the way (insert name) treated me (or is treating me). Help me to trust You and to believe You can and will use it to bring good into my life. Help me to give up my "right" to be resentful, and to forgive them as You have forgiven me. Amen.

Reflect

1. Write down any hurtful circumstance, caused by someone else, that still hurts you to think about. Spend time prayerfully committing the list to God. Ask Him to redeem every hurt and use it to bring good into your life. Ask for His help in forgiving those who have hurt you.
2. If you can at this time, ask God to bless and bring good to the person who hurt you (see Matthew 5:44).
3. Think of ways God has already used the mistreatment you suffered for your good. If you are using this book in a group study, take turns sharing about the good that God has brought into your lives.

God did not obliterate evil; He caused it to serve a higher purpose.

— Oswald Chambers, *My Utmost for His Highest*

What About Satan?
What About Our Choices?

I like routine, so I jog the same route every time; I have for six years, never varying. I know where all the ruts are. I know where the road goes uphill and where it's downhill. I know where the shade trees are. I know where there are sprinklers to run through on hot days. And, I know where all the dogs are!

I know which dogs are friendly, which ones are sleepy and which ones are mean. I know the one that is behind a big fence who runs along with me, barking and growling, and I know the one who always walks slowly toward me, wagging his tail.

I also know the one that is vicious and kept on a chain in the front yard. This one runs at me barking and snarling every time I run by. He always comes to the end of his chain before reaching me, but he keeps lunging and growling until I am well past him.

It took time to get used to him, but eventually he ceased to startle me. Then I began to think he was stupid not to recognize me after all the times I had passed by. One day as I was running along toward the yard where he was chained, I saw him start his usual charge at me, barking and snarling with his teeth bared. But this day as I casually looked over I noticed something else: he was not on his chain!

As the dog continued to run toward me, this time unimpeded by a chain, I immediately dropped and scrambled to clutch a rock, coming back up with broken fingernails and a handful of gravel. As he came snarling into the road, I started yelling and threw my arm back, prepared to throw my pitiful arsenal at him. Fear created an anger that was evident in my reaction to him. As he came forward, I ran toward him until he backed down. Continuing to yell, I cautiously ran by, my heart pounding and legs shaking.

I shouted back at the house that their dog was loose and that it was stupid to let him run free, still so angry and scared I wanted to confront the dog's owners. But as I slowed to a walk a little farther on, my adrenaline stopped pumping, my heart quit pounding and I began to cry.

I often use my running time for communion with God, talking to Him and praising Him. Today, however, as I wiped away my tears, I lashed out at Him too, "Why did You let that happen? You know I'm afraid of that dog anyway!"

I walked on home and put it behind me, but that morning during my quiet time, God gently began to talk to me about the incident.

"The dog didn't hurt you, did he?"

"Well," I stubbornly muttered, "he could have."

"But he didn't," God repeated.

"He could have, though. He's vicious!" I clung to my indignation just a little longer.

"He didn't hurt you," God spoke firmly. "He just frightened you and when you stood your ground and threw rocks at him, he backed down."

"Wellllll, I guess."

"I just wanted you to see how Satan works."

"Ohhhh." Suddenly I understood what God was trying to show me.

Satan is just like that big dog, vicious and mean and wanting to hurt us, but his chain is held by God. We get used to him and don't think about him until he gets off that chain and comes at us. Then frightened, we begin to scramble for rocks and yell at God, "Can't You control him?!"

Yet when we stand against Satan with the Word of God, he can't harm us, no matter how much he barks and growls, no matter how vicious he seems. But how does he get off the chain and how can we trust a God who would let him off?

There is a real Satan. God's Word makes that very clear, and there are times God does pull back His protection and allow Satan's attack. He did with Job. Satan was not allowed to destroy Job, but he was allowed to bring horrible tragedy and pain into his life. It is interesting to note that God purposely selected Job, initiating the whole episode. But He didn't do it to punish him. We can see from His conversation with Satan that God was proud of Job. However, He was also ready to mature him. He wanted to deepen Job's faith, to deal with his pride in his own righteousness and to draw him into a closer relationship. At the same time God was creating a history of the events that would be used to bring wisdom and peace to the hearts of people throughout the ages.

There was a lot riding on the outcome of this "wager" between God and Satan regarding Job. Remember that God can always see ahead to the outcome of any "attack" He may allow.

God's ultimate purpose in any trial or circumstance He allows us to face is to deepen our relationship with Him. Some of the problems we face will be caused by satanic activity. However, when God allows Satan's attacks, it is never to hurt or punish us, but to draw us closer and to teach us His principles. He sees ahead to the victory, the lessons learned, the deepening of our faith and the creating of our own personal history of overcoming through faith in Christ.

He knows that the attack will make us run to Him, even if it's just to yell, "Why did you let this happen?" While we are coming to Him for answers, His will can be accomplished in our lives. He will be able to point to the gaps in our armor that have allowed Satan's arrows to penetrate and hurt us, gaps caused by sin or apathy.

God will also use those times to teach us His principles so we will be strengthened in our spiritual lives. Part of the maturity God wants to bring into our lives is in the area of spiritual warfare. God wants us to grasp our authority as believers and stand against Satan (see Ephesians 6:10-18), so there will be times when He allows Satan "off his leash" for the express purpose of training us in this principle.

God wants us to learn to "work" with Him by praying for His will to be done on earth. Part of our work is to stand against Satan's attacks on ourselves and others, and to push back the forces of darkness that grip people. As we learn to work with God, our prayers will make a difference in our lives and in the world around us.

Our responsibility in times of adversity will always be to seek God. Later in this book, we will explore acknowledging God in everything. Our acknowledgment of God is not a blind acceptance of circumstances, but seeking God in all things. When we do that, God will reveal to us those times when our problems are caused by satanic activity.

As God brings maturity into our lives, He will enable us to stand against Satan with the Word. We will know that we do not need to be afraid. He will never unleash His control upon Satan except to ultimately bring good into our lives. When we are living our lives submitted to God's care, we can trust in His divine protection.

For greater is He that is in us, than he that is in the world.

–1 John 4:4 (KJV)

With Him is strength and wisdom: the deceived and the deceiver are His.

–Job 12:16 (KJV)

* * *

I hung up the phone after talking with Sally and sat in thoughtful contemplation of her problem. She had such a difficult life: an unsaved husband, a rebellious child and no change in sight. She was praying and trying to find peace in the midst of the pain, but it was difficult because God hadn't brought or allowed this circumstance into her life. She had. She had married an unsaved man knowing it was wrong, and now she was reaping the bitter fruit.

Many times we can point to difficult situations and say, "I can't accept this and trust God. This came about because of the decision I made."

Some turmoil-filled, painful situations — rocky marriages, wayward children, health problems, financial pressures, career disasters — can be traced back to our sinful decisions, made in times of rebellion, willfulness or a shallow, indifferent relationship with God. We chose the path we are walking, so we say, "How can I accept this as being from God and trust Him to bring good when I caused this?" We weep bitter tears of remorse and anger at the fruit we bear.

However, we are not big enough to block God's plans for our lives. Every decision to say no to God, or to walk in our own will, does hinder His divine direction for us and His desire to bless our lives with good, but no past decision will ever stand in His way.

God simply moves ahead, turning that choice into the path that He will use to bring redemption into our lives and to accomplish His will in us.

Like clay in the hand of the potter, so are you in my hand.

–Jeremiah 18:6

God's ultimate will for you is an unhindered, unbroken relationship with Him. His spirit resides within you. When you are yielded to Him, you can enjoy abundant life and a divine love relationship with God.

Whenever you make the decision to live a yielded life, He simply takes the path you are on and begins to redeem that path, just as He redeems you. He can use it to accomplish His will in your life, and He can bring good from it. The rocky path that you have set your feet upon then becomes the very path God will use to bring you to the beauty of a mature, restored relationship with Him.

God is fully capable of blocking any path you may be on. If He does not, then you may rest assured it is not a path of destruction, but a path of redemption: a painful one, perhaps, maybe not the one God would have liked to have given you, but a path God can use for your good and His glory.

Perhaps the very aspects of your character that caused you to make those decisions necessitate a rockier path in order for God to bring healing to a scarred life, brokenness to a strong will or insight to blinded eyes. Whatever the reason, God does see ahead, to the results of our paths and to the redemptive work that will be accomplished in us: correction, healing, repentance, building, maturing and understanding.

Our heavenly Father is able to bring about all that is needed on the paths we are walking. He will not waste any part of it. He will use it all to accomplish His purpose in us. We can trust Him to bring good even out of our past.

Forget the former things; do not dwell on the past. See, I am doing a new thing! Now it springs up; do you not perceive it? I am making a way in the desert and streams in the wasteland.

– Isaiah 43:18-19

Repairing Lives

Even from my sin, God draws good.
— St. Augustine

Sometimes when we look at our lives and the messes we've made, it is easy to feel discouraged, but Christ, who is the redeemer of our lives, is determined to bring His good into every part. For those feeling defeated by the past, look up Isaiah 51:3. Write your name in the margin beside where it says "Zion." This is God's promise to you.

God delights in doing the impossible. He takes the ruined and broken and reshapes, retools and brings forth incredible beauty. It's one of the things He does best. It is what He will do with your life.

Study

What promise does God give you in Isaiah 43:1-3,5?

____

____

What instruction does He give in Isaiah 43:18-19?

____

____

Read Psalm 139:1-4. What kind of knowledge does God have?

____

Why are we assured of victory over Satan's attacks? See Job 12:16 and John 19:11. ________________________________

____

Look up Isaiah 58:11-12 and meditate on these verses. In light of the truths from this chapter, what do these Scriptures mean to you?

____

____

Memorize

The Lord will guide you always.
Isaiah 58:11

Prayer of Response

Dear heavenly Father, I am struggling with regret over the choices I made in the past. The repercussions often seem more than I can bear. But I believe that even though you did not choose this path for me, You are able to redeem my choices, and that even in this — You can bring good. I ask for Your help in submitting myself to You and allowing Your work of redemption in these circumstances. Amen.

Reflect

Think about St. Augustine's words on the previous page. From what in your life, that could be called "sin," has God brought good?

Extra Weight

"I bought you something," Chuck announced one evening when he walked in the door from work.

"Oh, what is it?" I asked as I turned away from the potatoes I was peeling for dinner to see what he had brought. I love surprises, especially flowers for no special reason. However, I saw immediately it wasn't flowers he was holding, but a shopping bag from his favorite sporting goods store. Suddenly I didn't have such a good feeling about this surprise.

I walked over and took the bag. My arm immediately dropped from the weight. "What's in here?" I asked as I opened it to look in. At the bottom of the bag were two funny-looking pieces of metal with grip tape around part of them. I looked up with a puzzled expression.

"They're hand weights," he explained.

When my expression didn't change, he continued, "You carry them when you jog."

"Okay…and why would I want to do that?"

"They are supposed to maximize your workout so that you use more energy in less amount of time."

Chuck had been thrilled when I started jogging and he was always trying to encourage me to run farther and faster, talking to me about wind sprints and pace and 8-minute miles. He tried to talk me into running a marathon with him and I started the training, but after a month I finally told him I didn't want to spend that much time training for something I had no interest in doing except to please him.

I thought he understood, but as I looked at the weights, it was obvious he was still trying to help me be a better runner.

He explained a little more about the principle involved. It did sound like a good idea, so I dutifully agreed to try them the next day.

When I walked out of the house early the following morning, I picked up the little metal bars and started out. They only weighed four pounds a piece and at first I felt pretty cool running with them, but after only a couple of blocks my heart was racing and I was huffing and puffing.

I ran a few more blocks, but my steps began to drag. Resolutely, I tried to keep going, struggling to put one foot in front of the other (in my mind I could hear Chuck advising, "Run through the pain!") but I wasn't even halfway through my normal route, when I realized I would never make it. My back was hurting, my arms were aching and I was furious at Chuck for talking me into trying it.

I started walking, but even walking with them was hard. They were so heavy that I longed to put them down. It was funny, they hadn't seemed heavy when I started but now they were pulling on my arms like huge millstones. I could have sworn I was carrying around hundreds of pounds instead of eight.

I thought about throwing them in some bushes and leaving them but instead I cut my route short and headed home, concentrating on putting one foot in front of the other. By the time I got home I was exhausted. I laid the weights down and looked at them, thinking, *Why would I want to do this every day?* Immediately a Scripture popped into my mind: "Let us lay aside every weight, and the sin which so easily ensnares us, and let us run with endurance the race that is set before us." (Hebrews 12:1 NKJV)

Never before had that Scripture been so alive to me. What a difference just a little extra weight had made in my run that morning, and what a relief it had been to lay it down! Then I thought about the other "weight" I routinely carried around. That morning as God again spoke to my heart about it, I saw with fresh insight the unnecessary toll it was taking on my life.

The weight that I allowed to burden my days and torment my nights is the same weight that many others carry. Constantly, it weighs us down and keeps us exhausted and unable to live a victorious Christian life ("the race that is set before us"). Circumstances keep us in turmoil, setbacks demoralize us, problems overwhelm us, fear constantly grips us and we, who as Christians should live lives of peace and joy, are instead beset by the weights of worry and fear. Proverbs 12:25 says it perfectly: "An anxious heart weighs a man down."

What is the answer to our tendency to carry extra weight? For me, the answer was simple. I just gave the weights back to Chuck and said, "These aren't for me, thank you." But for many of us it's as if the weights are permanently glued to our hands and we cannot seem to get rid of them. We mistakenly believe if we worry enough we can control our problems. We've lived with worry, anxiety and fear for so long, we don't know what to do with them or how to get rid of them.

The answer, of course, is in learning to trust God. If you have decided that God "is the blessed controller of all things," then at some point that belief is going to have to make a difference in your life. It is going to have to make a difference in the way you react to the situations you face.

What makes you anxious? What do you worry over? Money? Your health? Your children or grandchildren? The condition of the world? Your job? The "worry list" can be endless!

Anxiety is never God's will for us, so before we go any farther in our journey to "trust," we need to begin to learn to apply the principle that is the theme for the first section of this book: God is the blessed controller of all things. Your life, your family's lives and your future are in His hands. There will be good and bad in your future, but God is always in control. Not only is He in control but He promises that in all things He works for the good of those who love Him.

If you are not going to be controlled by your circumstances or the tyranny of the "what ifs," you are going to have to make those truths a part of your day-by-day, moment-by-moment, life. That means consciously, day by day, in those moments when fear grips you, choosing to remember that God is in control. It may mean bringing your thoughts back into line with that truth over and over.

When I first began to learn the lessons of trust, I constantly spoke the phrase "God is the blessed controller of all things" to myself. My friends and I began to speak it to each other, and when I came to God in prayer I spoke to Him, "God, I know You are the blessed controller of all things." Gradually, that truth began to become a part of my life, freeing me from the weights of fear and worry.

* * *

Although fear or worry are the most obvious weights we may carry around when we fail to believe in God's control and ability to bring good from our lives, there are other weights that can drag us down in our walk with God. Believing God is the blessed controller of all things is the answer to much of the mental turmoil we find ourselves in, such as:

- *Regret.* In looking back, we often wrestle with this feeling: "if only," as in "if only it had been different." You know those moments on which you wish you had a second chance to act? "If only I had done this" or "if only I had thought of that" — if only, if only, if only. Over and over, we try to rewrite the scenarios in our minds to recreate the outcomes. Some people are more prone to the "what ifs" than others, but the answer for all of us is in letting go of the regret and trusting that God is the blessed controller of all things — even the details of our lives that we overlook. God knows your path and He will bring good from everything that touches your life.
- *Responsibility.* Many of us suffer from the curse of feeling too responsible for what happens around us. We feel if we can just take care of all the details, we can make everyone happy. Of course, this kind of underlying motivation sets us up for a great deal of frustration, disappointment and pain.

* * *

Perhaps the "weight" you've been carrying around is not fear, worry or regret. Instead, your pain is caused by the fact that you do believe God is the blessed controller of all things. You believe He could have prevented your circumstances, but He didn't. Part of you is still so bitter because of the pain you've been forced to endure that you don't want anything good from the God who allowed it into your life.

Maybe you haven't thought it through to that extent, but underneath your pain is a basic anger at God that stems from the root of self which says, "I shouldn't be treated this way. How could you, God?!" Like a child, you are pulling away from the very one who can help you;

pulling away from the God who loves you and only wants good for you.

The next step for you in your journey of learning to trust God is letting go of the anger by making a conscious decision to do so. It will have to begin with an acknowledgment to God that the anger is there and you can't get rid of it yourself. That step should enable you to take the next one, which is asking God to help you let go of the anger. This will enable the Holy Spirit to unleash His ability to help you forgive God. Then you can begin to allow God to bring His good into your life.

Putting Down the Weight

Have you accepted God's sovereignty over your circumstances and yet your life is still lacking peace and joy? Has the truth of God as the blessed controller of all things made a difference in your tendency to worry? What about your tendency to regret or to shoulder too much responsibility? Are you struggling with feelings of anger at God for not keeping you from the pain you are experiencing today? Wherever you are in your personal journey to trust in God, it may be time to really look at the extra weight you are carrying, resolving to lay it down today.

Study

What small thing does God clothe and take care of (Matthew 6:25-34)?

____

What is a small detail of your life under God's control (Matthew 10:30)?

____

Read Isaiah 40:12-31. These Scriptures are God's answer to Israel's complaint in verse 27. It is a reminder of God's omnipotence and power. What tiny item does God measure (v. 12)? ________________

____

____

Look up 1 Timothy 6:15. Underline the Scripture, then write the phrase "blessed controller of all things" in the margin. Continue to meditate on this Scripture and let all of its truth begin to permeate your life.

List the things for which you have been worrying, regretting or feeling too responsible. Talk to God about each thing and ask Him to forgive you and change your thinking patterns so they reflect the truth about Him, His control, His goodness and His trustworthiness.

____

____

____

Each day, begin to ask God to bring your every thought into line with these truths:

God is the blessed controller of all things.

God can be trusted with all of my life.

God is good all of the time.

Memorize

Finally, brothers, whatever is true, whatever is noble, whatever is right, whatever is pure, whatever is lovely, whatever is admirable — if anything is excellent or praiseworthy — think about such things.

Phillipians 4:8

Prayer of Response

Dear heavenly Father, please help me today. I submit myself to You and I ask You to free me from the things that weigh me down and keep me from walking in peace, joy and trust in Your goodness. Forgive me for hanging onto the weight of ________________. Show me how to lay it down. I want to learn to trust You. Help me to learn to trust every part of my life to You and to believe that You are good all the time. Amen.

Reflect

1. What kinds of circumstances cause you to worry the most?
2. How much time do you spend worrying?
3. How do you think God views your worry?

Part Two

Lean Not on Your Own Understanding

My Understanding

It seems the more we come to believe in and accept the sovereignty of God over every event of our lives, the more we are tempted to question His love. We think, "If God is in control of this adversity and can do something about it, why doesn't He?"

— Jerry Bridges, *Trusting God*

Learning that God is the blessed controller of all things is a wonderful beginning to the path to trust in God, but it is only the beginning. Believing God is in control won't always be enough to stop the confusion, the questioning, the worry and the pain that life seems to bring.

We may have adopted this foundation, but unfortunately we are still at the mercy of our own understanding, and our understanding will always bring questioning and fear. It is hard to understand God and His ways. Accepting the truth in our hearts about God's control of our circumstances isn't always enough to stop the turmoil of our thinking. So the next step in our path to trust in God is learning to replace our perspectives with God's perspective — giving up our understanding and taking hold of His.

...And lean not on your own understanding.

– Proverbs 3:5

* * *

I love April Fool's Day. I always have. My children still endure the jokes and tricks I play on them, usually early in the morning before they remember what day it is. But I'm gentle with my pranks, always remembering another April Fool's Day…

My girlfriend and I laughed and chattered all the way home from high school about the fun stuff that had gone on that day and about what we could do to trick someone at my house.

By the time we got home, we had come up with a great idea. We put our books away, got a snack and went to my bedroom to plan. When no one was looking, we got a bottle of ketchup out of the refrigerator and put it in the garage. We found an empty glass jar and put it with the ketchup, then waited.

About 5:00, when my mother started dinner, we casually walked past her in the kitchen and into the garage. I muttered something about needing stuff for a project. Noisily, I dragged the ladder from the backyard into the garage, saying through the back window, "I've got to get something."

In the garage, I quickly covered myself with ketchup, climbed up to the top of the ladder and threw the glass jar down onto the concrete floor. Then, screaming at the top of my lungs, I jumped down and fell on the ground.

My mother was out the kitchen door before I hit the ground, screaming, "Oh, my baby! OH NO, MY BABY!!!"

She ran to me with the most anguished expression I had ever seen. By the time she reached me, the look on her face had overwhelmed any feelings of fun over the prank, and I sort of weakly said, "April Fools???"

She stopped and just stared at me for a few seconds as if trying to grasp what I had said. Then she burst into tears and ran back into the house.

I looked at my friend. Her expression, I'm sure, mirrored mine. It was a look of bewilderment and chagrin. Quietly, we started cleaning up the mess, feeling terrible. Then my dad came out. When he finished with us, we felt even worse. After apologizing to my mother, we went to my room and tried to figure out what went wrong. We hadn't meant any harm. Mom loved a good joke as much as anyone. It had never occurred to me that this wouldn't be funny to her. I just hadn't thought about the joke from her perspective.

That memory still bothers me. I still regret frightening my mother that badly, especially now that I have children of my own and I understand the kind of overwhelmingly protective love and concern a mother feels for her children.

It was a foolish thing to do, but as a kid, I didn't know that. I would never do something like that now because my perspective has changed. I can see past the "joke" and understand the consequences.

How often do we as Christians look at circumstances without being able to see past our own perspectives? Like non-thinking teenagers or immature children, we act as if our feelings, thoughts and opinions about situations and people are all that matters.

After we accept Christ and begin to learn some biblical principles, we often think we understand God's ways. But usually we still look at situations, people and God Himself with childish eyes. We don't realize we're doing so — our ignorance and lack of spiritual insight are hidden from us by our "own understanding."

We make decisions based on our own wisdom and we hold opinions about God based upon very limited knowledge. We look at situations and people through eyes totally blind to God's perspective...and find it hard to trust Him. But if we are going to be able to trust God, then we are going to have to understand His ways, and take hold of His thoughts, His insights, His values, and His perception of the world in which we live.

We "see" from the perspectives of our own lives, our backgrounds, our personalities, our likes and dislikes and our desires and hopes. This isn't wrong. However, it is tremendously limited. At the same time, our "understanding" is seriously distorted by the sin heritage into which we were born. When you add the fact that our understanding is also filtered through the "I" that has been at the center of our lives for so long, it will perhaps be easier to see why God tells us "lean not unto your own understanding." In "our understanding," we need for things to go our way in order for us to feel good about life, ourselves and God — and thus be able to trust Him.

Before I became a Christian, my understanding was limited to how well "I" was doing in my circumstances that day. Is life going well? Do "I" have enough money? Are "my" relationships satisfying my needs?

When we accept Christ, God puts His Spirit in us. As His divine life flows through us, we have access to "His" understanding. However, because learning God's ways and receiving His understanding is a process that takes time, we continue to be hindered by our own understanding. We still base our well-being on "how well am I doing?" As we face the problems, the discouragement, the heartache and the questioning that are part of human life, we are unable to rest and trust in God because our understanding is in the way.

What is the answer to this problem of "our understanding"? From where will the trust needed for new understanding come? Is it only a matter of maturing by learning more of God's Word and spending more time in prayer?

* * *

A friend called the other day to complain about the way God was treating her. The first thing she said was "I never know if God's going to answer my prayers or not. I feel like I'm always having to make excuses for Him when He doesn't."

Then she told me about the problem she and her husband were having in selling their house because his job transfer was moving them to another town. They were facing the possibility of not being able to buy a house in the new town and having to make double payments while they rented.

"Why can't God just take care of it?" she went on to say. "It would build my faith so much. I'm always amazed and grateful when He answers my prayers, and it really does build my faith and trust. How can I tell people God is taking care of situations if I don't know if He will?"

I tried to encourage her by reminding her that God was in control and that He was responsible for His own name and honor, but after we hung up I thought about her words. If God's coming through for her was the way to build her faith and trust, why was she having such a hard time trusting Him now? He had helped her many, many times in the past. Hadn't those times of deliverance and help been enough to build her faith and her relationship with God?

But, in moments of fear and discouragement, past experiences of deliverance aren't always enough.

Many years ago, God performed miracle after miracle to free the Hebrews from Pharaoh's grip in Egypt. The awesome plagues He inflicted upon Egypt while He protected them, and their deliverance from slavery through His miraculous intervention, certainly should have enabled the Israelites to trust God when they came to the Red Sea.

But instead, they cried out in fear, "Was it because there were no graves in Egypt that you brought us here to die?"

* * *

Like the Israelites, you and I struggle with our questions. We struggle with our doubts, and we struggle with our inability to trust God. We say things like, "I know God will take care of this, but I wish He would hurry," or "I just can't see how God can bring good out of THIS!" or "God just doesn't seem to hear me."

Even God's Word doesn't always help us. Sometimes when we're anxious over circumstances, someone will quote a Scripture like, "My God shall supply all your needs." Annoyed, we think, *I already know that Scripture, but I'm still broke.*

* * *

Stressful circumstances have a way of showing very quickly how far we've really come in learning to trust God. When past deliverances don't seem to help, when knowledge of God's Word doesn't bring peace, when we spend our days in turmoil, fear and bitterness — then we are still leaning on our own understanding. "Our understanding" will not bring peace in the middle of the storm. We are not deep enough into a divine relationship with God to enable us to get past our own emotions and fearful appraisal of the problems.

God knows what kind of circumstances will make us turn from contentment to murmuring, thereby revealing the true state of our trust in Him. Often it only takes a little extra nudge in a situation — God taking just a little longer than we think He should, something not going the way we want — and we begin to murmur, complain and wallow in self-pity. We blame our spouse, our past, Satan, the economy or the weather for the mess we're in. We take matters into our own hands, and we fail to trust God.

* * *

The Israelite nation had the same problem.

They, like us, had been delivered from sin's curse. God had delivered them from slavery in Egypt. They were grateful and ready to be His chosen people, but within hours they came upon the Red Sea. With Pharaoh's armies at their backs and a perilous sea in front of them, they suddenly forgot their desire to be His people. Instead, they cried out in confusion and fear. And even though God delivered them with a mighty miracle, the real problem remained: they didn't know Him. They didn't know who He was, what He would do or what He wanted from them. They still didn't know if they could trust Him.

So God planned a journey for them, a journey through the wilderness. A journey in which they would have to depend upon Him. A journey in which He could reveal Himself to them, and a journey that would lead them away from their own understanding to God's.

Their destination was Canaan. There they would dwell as God's chosen people, enjoying His blessing, protection and love. They wouldn't be free of battles and problems, but because of the journey, they would know God's principles, God's ways and, most importantly, they would know Him.

I am the Lord, who makes you holy and who brought you out of Egypt to be your God.

–Leviticus 22:32-33

Before entering Canaan, the Israelites had to learn to rely on God in the wilderness. He placed them in situations that were frightening, but He always delivered them from their enemies. They endured hardships, but He always took care of their physical needs.

They were not always sure where they were going or when they would get there, but He always provided daily direction.

In all things, God was revealing Himself to the children of Israel — who He was and what He was like — so they could know and trust Him.

At the same time, God began to give them principles to live by. He instructed them in His requirements for righteousness. He revealed their sinfulness to them and He provided atonement. He instituted worship and showed them the way into His presence!

You and I, like the children of Israel, will not really learn to know God until our knowledge of God's trustworthiness is put to the test of stressful circumstances. We learn to know and trust God not when everything goes our way and God seems to be doing a great job of taking care of us, but when circumstances seem to say that God has forgotten us — our bank account is in the red, our best friend betrays us, our child runs away from home, we face a life-threatening illness — and suddenly, we enter the wilderness.

There we learn to know God in the same way the Israelites did: through day-by-day life, through Red Sea experiences and through His Word becoming a part of our lives. God longs to have a relationship with us. He desires a close, loving, interdependent relationship — one in which our love and devotion to Him is based on who He is, not what He does for us.

Our desire for God changes along with our emotions and needs. However, He wants to mature us past that. He wants to show us what a real relationship is like, giving us the peace, joy and trust in Him that we want, but aren't sure how to get.

When God holds back His hand of blessing or deliverance during difficult times, He is drawing us to seek Him, not His hand. He desires a change of focus in what we are pursuing, so that we realize we aren't getting what we're crying out for and hopefully we'll learn to cry out for Him, His presence and His sustenance.

Turmoil, problems and pain seem to be the only way our attention can be torn away from our pursuit of taking care of ourselves, and all that entails, to confronting larger realities: the reality of who we are and the reality of who God is. Is God good? Is He trustworthy? Does He help me? Will He deliver me from this pain, this mess? Will I love Him if He doesn't? Do I really want to "know" Him?

Each of us will, at some point, enter into our own personal wilderness journeys. Each will encompass unique situations and different emphases. But with each of us, God's goal is the same: to cause us to come to the end of ourselves, so we will be ready to seek Him; to lead us away from Egypt by teaching us to move away from our own distorted windows of understanding; and to enable us to see through His understanding.

Take my yoke upon you and learn from me...and you will find rest for your souls.

– Matthew 11:29

Changing Focus

The Bible's accounts show that miracles — dramatic, show-stopping miracles like many of us still long for — simply do not foster deep faith.
— Philip Yancey

I still want answers — sometimes more than I want God.
— Dr. Larry Crabb, *Finding God*

Are you demanding answers today? Are you insisting on deliverance from your problems as proof of God's love? Are you having difficulty getting past your understanding so that you can trust God?

Our questioning and our bewilderment at God's seeming lack of help in the middle of problems is natural, but it may be time to let go of the demanding. It may be time to ask God to help you want Him more than you want answers.

This kind of attitude doesn't come naturally. It won't come without submission on your part. Today, wrench your eyes away from whatever is consuming you and look to God for help in gaining a new perspective.

Study

Read Psalm 147:5. How does this verse describe God's understanding?

____

Read Job 28:20-24. What is the difference between your understanding and God's? ______________________________

Read Jeremiah 17:9-10. What problem do people have that affect our understanding? ____________________________________

What does Isaiah 55:8-9 say about our thoughts and God's?

____

____

____

What reason does Proverbs 20:24 give for man's lack of understanding? ____________________________________

____

____

Read Psalm 147:5. What word(s) are used to describe God's understanding? ____________________________________

____

Read Isaiah 40:27. What did the Israelites say about God that mirrors our attitude during difficult times? ____________________

____

____

This week, read Exodus, chapters 6 through 17. On a separate sheet of paper, list the miracles God performed on behalf of the Israelites, using these Scriptures from Exodus:

- 7:19-21
- 8:5-6
- 8:16-17
- 8:21-24
- 9:2-6
- 9:8-10
- 9:22-26
- 10:12-15
- 10:21-23
- 12:29-30

How did God lead the children of Israel? (Exodus 13:21)

____

____

What was the Israelites' response when they saw the Egyptian armies behind them and the Red Sea in front of them? (Exodus 14:10)

____

____

Memorize

For my thoughts are not your thoughts, neither are your ways my ways, declares the Lord. As the heavens are higher than the earth, so are my ways higher than your ways and my thoughts than your thoughts.
Isaiah 55:8-9

Prayer of Response

Father God, I confess that right now I do want answers more than I want You. The problem seems so big and all-consuming that relief from it has become more important than You. I ask for Your help in letting go of this attitude. I ask You to help me to trust You. Amen.

Reflect

1. What is your perspective on what has happened or is happening to you right now?
2. What has been your response to the armies (painful circumstances) and Red Seas (problems) that are in your life?
3. Think about some of the deliverances and help you have received from God in the past.

Crickets

A few years ago we made a trip to a nearby town for my niece's graduation. My parents live in that town, so we stopped at their house to change clothes before heading over to the graduation ceremony. We were running late so we rushed in and immediately dispersed to bedrooms and bathrooms to change. My mom followed me into the bathroom where I was combing my hair. As we were chatting, I kept hearing an odd sound.

"What's that noise, Mom?" I asked.

"That's those crickets," she answered. "Remember? I told you about them."

"Ohhh yes, I remember."

She had told me about them, several times in fact, during our phone conversations over the last month. She and Dad had been struggling to find the crickets which seemed to be infesting their house.

"I don't know what we're going to do," she continued, frustration evident in her voice. "We just can't seem to find them."

"Well, it sounds like it's coming from the hall, Mom."

"Oh, they're in every room," she answered. "No matter what room you're in you can hear them and…well, I finally asked my prayer group to help me pray about it. If we can't get rid of them, they are going to start multiplying. They could begin to eat the drapes and…"

"But it sure sounds like it's coming from right out here," I interrupted as I walked out of the bathroom into the hall to listen. My son, Matthew, came out of one of the bedrooms at that time and both of us stood listening.

After a moment I said, "Uh, Mom. I think I know where your crickets are."

She came out to the hall with a smile of indulgence and said, "Oh, honey, we've been looking for weeks."

"No, Mom, you don't understand." I pointed to the smoke detector on the ceiling in the hall. "The battery in your smoke alarm needs replaced. That cricket is the warning sound."

My mother just shook her head with her don't-try-and-tell-your-mother-something-you-know-nothing-about look and proceeded to remind me that she could hear them all over the house. "I know we've got crickets, Deb. They're in every room, not just the hall."

"Well, every room is connected to this hall," I answered.

Matt began timing the "crickets" on his watch. Sure enough, they chirped every 21 seconds on the dot.

When my dad came into the hall and we told him we'd found his crickets, he laughed, shook his head and gave us the same look Mom had. But as Matthew proceeded to time the "crickets" with perfect accuracy over and over again, showing his grandfather his watch as he did, you could see the realization begin to dawn.

My capable and intelligent dad just harrumphed and walked away, embarrassed to be caught not knowing something as simple as that. My mom was more incredulous. You could tell she still didn't know if she believed it. She had lived with the idea of crickets for so long she couldn't believe it could be something else, but when Chuck changed the battery in the smoke alarm, the "crickets" were silenced.

My parents had turned their house upside-down looking for those crickets, assuming they were moving from room to room. My mom had even asked her prayer group to pray about the invasion of crickets! How many times do we do the same thing? We have a problem and we look at our circumstances and say, "I need to get rid of these crickets!" We begin to pray, "Lord, help us to find the crickets. Oh, God, help us get rid of the crickets!"

All the time we're praying, we don't have a clue as to what our real problem is. We don't see that our real problem isn't what seems to be staring us in the face. Our real problem is that we don't trust God. Unfortunately, when we are in the middle of a trial we don't see it as a test of our faith. It is just something we want out of — anything to stop the pain, end the turmoil and fix the problem. We don't see that our real problem is our "own understanding," our faulty perception of God and our mistrust of Him.

After crossing the Red Sea, the Israelites soon came to the Springs of Elim. There were 12 springs and 70 palm trees. What a great place! I'm sure many thought it would be wonderful to stay there. Why go on? They had all they needed right there. The children of Israel didn't really want to walk through the wilderness — neither do we!

Why doesn't God let us stay by the springs? Why doesn't He answer our prayers as we'd like and take care of all our problems for us? Like my friend said, "Why can't He just take care of it?" That's what we need! If we could just count on Him to wrap up every loose end and make us well and happy, our cars would always run right, our kids would all have straight teeth, our roofs would never leak and tragedy would never touch our lives. Then we could really trust God!

If that's all it would take, why doesn't God work that way? He could. Any computer-like God could carry out all our wishes and make everything nice. But would we be happy if we always had the money we needed, were never sick and never had bad things happen to us? Would we be happy staying at Elim?

Unfortunately, no. With our sinful distorted natures, that would not be nearly enough. God would be forever protecting us from the many problems our distorted natures produce.

God is doing much more in us than just taking care of our needs. He knows that we were created for a God-centered life and nothing short of that will bring us true happiness. He knows that our own self-directed natures will lead us quickly away from Him, back to Egypt.

The problem is where our trust really lies. It is in ourselves. So He must force us to come to the end of ourselves so that we will begin to seek Him. He must wrest from us our tightly-held perceptions of security and happiness and teach us that real security and real happiness are in God Himself.

God delights in giving us good things, in blessing us and delivering us from problems. But there are times that will come for all of us when He wants our faith and trust in Him to take root and be based not on our physical experiences of well-being, but on our spirits well-being. God wants to change the carnal nature that gets us into so much trouble and to refocus our sight so that we begin to see as He does. A child who is always carried will never learn to walk. A Christian who never faces adversity will never learn to know and trust God.

And we rejoice in the hope of the glory of God. Not only so, but we also rejoice in our sufferings, because we know that suffering produces perseverance; perseverance, character; and character, hope.

–Romans 5:3-4

Our troubles bring us to Jesus. It is as simple as that. We would like to think we would seek His face and His will in our lives on our own, but that just doesn't happen – at least not until a maturing process has taken place in our lives. And even though maturing seems to happen best in the wilderness, we hate it. Everything in us screams, "Why, God? It hurts! It's uncomfortable! It's demeaning! It takes too long!"

We seem to be so blind to our own need for growth and change that we seldom understand what God is trying to accomplish with the pressures, stresses and painful circumstances He allows to come our way on our "journey to Canaan." We still think we have "crickets"!

Our understanding is "Things are okay. I'm not so bad. I love God, go to church, teach a class…" or even "I'm in full-time ministry for God!" — until circumstances force us to confront Red Seas and golden calves. In desperation, we see that our understanding isn't enough anymore. We must look for His.

The Israelites' journey seemed to be one crisis after another. They were constantly getting into predicaments that tried their fledgling faith. Yet God did not bring them to the brink of disaster simply to see them squirm and panic. His purpose was not to say, "I knew you'd blow it!" Each time the people of Israel were helpless to save themselves, they were then in a position to lean upon God and learn that He would take care of them. He was able to build their faith, expose their sinfulness, point out their neediness and draw them close as He revealed Himself to them. That is what God wanted.

Their wilderness journey put the children of Israel in the position of having to seek God, or rebel. Either way, they were in a position where God could deal with them. They, like us, were guilty of apathy toward God when things were going well. After their deliverance from Egypt, they would have liked to have been left alone. Yet God knew that left to themselves, they would soon be in bondage to some other taskmaster.

God had to show the Israelites what was in them before He could show them what He would do for them. In the wilderness, they were forced to confront God. In our own wildernesses we will be forced to, also. When all else is bleak, we have to decide to either rebel or lean upon God.

We do not need deliverance from bad circumstances in order to be content — we need deliverance from ourselves. This is deliverance from our own understanding, our deeply-rooted preoccupation with self that gets us in trouble over and over and keeps us from trusting God unless things are going our way!

Popular Christian speaker Bill Gothard says, "Wisdom is seeing as God sees." When we lean on God's understanding instead of our own, we receive God's sight. If we look at all of the circumstances of our lives, from major crises to petty disappointments, as being orchestrated by God to teach us, to reveal truth to us and to change us, then we are ready to see as God sees. We have ceased to lean upon our own understanding and begun to lean upon His.

We were created for fellowship with God. We were created to be inhabited and directed by His Spirit. God knows that no other kind of life will bring us true happiness. No other kind of life will fulfill our need for communion with God, and it will never fulfill God's desire for a relationship with us.

Consider it pure joy, my brothers, whenever you face trials of many kinds, because you know that the testing of your faith develops perseverance. Perseverance must finish its work so that you may be mature and complete, not lacking anything.

–James 1:2-4

A New Understanding

How many times have I heard from those who have endured intense suffering that the experience of their pain has cured them of the idolatries that once robbed them of joy. The father who abandons us, the spouse who leaves us, the financial catastrophe that ruins us, the rude interruption of our plans, the revelation of a horrifying illness, the painful, prolonged dealing — all escalate our love for God. All are His ways of prying our fingers from things that are false and that will not satisfy. They pull us away from lesser loves and enlarge our intimacy with our Shepherd, which is what brings us peace and unimaginable joy.

— David Roper, *Psalm 23*

Do you remain in a turmoil of everyday stresses and problems? Do you see every bad thing that happens as an affront to your rights? Have you refused to look at your problems with any kind of awareness that God has perhaps allowed them for spiritual purposes? Are there any "crickets" in your life from which you have been asking God to deliver you?

It may be difficult to change your way of thinking about your problems, but perhaps it's time to allow God to give you a new understanding of them. You may never fully understand some tragedies. However, it may be time to look at your problems with a fresh awareness, seeing that they may have been allowed to bring new growth and maturity, new insight into your own character, new awareness of your sin nature and new knowledge of God Himself.

Study

Read Psalm 95:10. What seems to go along with not understanding God's ways? ____

What does Deuteronomy 8:15-16 say is the reason God led the

Israelites through the wilderness? ______________________

What happened to Israel when things went well for them (Hosea 13:6)?

____

Read 1 Corinthians 2:13-16. What keeps us from spiritual understanding? (v. 14) ______________________

However, what do you and I have? (v. 16) ______________________

What does 1 Corinthians 1:30 say is one of the things Christ is to us?

____

What other gift enables us to receive spiritual understanding? (1 Corinthians 2:10; 1 John 2:20)______________________

What does John 16:13 say about this gift that indicates that receiving new understanding and knowledge is a process? ______________________

____

____

Memorize

Do not conform any longer to the pattern of this world, but be transformed by the renewing of your mind. Then you will be able to test and approve what God's will is — his good, pleasing and perfect will.
Romans 12:2

Prayer of Response

Father, just like the Israelites, I have been guilty of apathy toward You when things are going well. Please forgive me for this tendency and help me to desire You wholeheartedly. I do want to know You, Father, and spend time with You. I need Your help, dear Holy Spirit, to respond faithfully to my Father's call to intimacy. Place a longing in my heart for fellowship and a desire to know God better. Amen.

Reflect

1. What circumstance has God used to pry your fingers away from false things?
2. Can you let go of your own understanding and allow God to work through you? If you are struggling, offer this prayer:

   Dear Father, I realize that in order to trust You, I have to stop leaning on my understanding and my natural way of looking at things. I know that through Jesus I have access to Your wisdom and understanding. Help me to receive it and to rely on the Holy Spirit every day for Your understanding. Amen.

Is It Good or Is It Bad?

There is an old Chinese parable about a farmer with one son and a horse. One night the son left the gate open to the corral where the horse was kept. During the night, the horse got out and ran away.

The next morning, the farmer saw the open gate and the empty enclosure. As he was standing there, his neighbor came over to commiserate with him about his loss. "Oh, oh, this is terrible," he said, "This is so bad."

The farmer was quiet for a moment before answering, "How do you know it's bad?"

"What do you mean?" his neighbor exclaimed. "Of course it's bad!"

The farmer didn't say anything else. Finally, his neighbor walked away, shaking his head.

Early the next morning, as the sun came up over the horizon, the son looked out the window and saw their horse running toward the farm. Following him was a whole herd of horses. He yelled to his father and quickly ran out to open the gate to the corral.

In ran the horse with all of the wild horses behind him. He shut the gate and turned to his father with a huge grin.

Later that day, the neighbor heard what happened and came over to congratulate the farmer.

"What good fortune!" he exclaimed. "This is really a good thing that's happened to you."

But the farmer simply answered, "How do you know it's good?"

"Well, of course it's good." Pointing at the horses, the neighbor tried to share the farmer's good fortune, but he realized after looking into the farmer's expressionless face that he wasn't celebrating. The neighbor walked away, shaking his head again.

The next morning, the son turned to his father and said, "These horses can bring us a lot of money. I'm going to go out and break some of them so we can sell them."

He headed out to the enclosure, but while he was working with the horses one of them knocked him against the fence, breaking both of his legs. His father took him to the village infirmary.

When he returned to the farm, his neighbor was standing outside the corral.

"Oh, my, I heard what happened," he said. "That is too bad."

The farmer replied, "How do you know it's bad?"

The neighbor didn't try to argue this time.

The very next day, the emperor's warlords came marching through the village and conscripted all able-bodied young men into the army. The farmer's son was in the infirmary with two broken legs and couldn't be taken.

When the neighbor came over to see the farmer, he said, "Oh, what good fortune for you."

Of course, the farmer answered, "How do you know?"

How do we know what's good?

How do we know what's bad?

In an earlier chapter, I shared about Bob Benson's retreat prayer times, where he asked participants to write down the good and bad events of their lives. It was interesting how many of them, in looking back at events that seemed terrible at one time, were forced to change their minds about the events because time had altered their perceptions.

Time can do that. But while it is true that time often changes our perceptions or understanding of events, it doesn't always…at least not on its own. Time itself isn't the answer for Christians. There's more to it than that. More than time is needed if we are to exchange our understanding for God's and see as He sees.

What do we do while we are in the middle of a circumstance that is damaging to our trust? Can we learn to see differently while we are in the middle of a problem? We have such temporal, carnal views of life that it is difficult to be aware of God's overriding care when we are in the middle of hurtful circumstances. It is only through exchanging our understanding for God's that we will begin to see with any kind of spiritual perspective and be able to exchange our anxiety for trust in God.

But how does this exchange take place? How do we finally begin to move away from the distortions, half-truths and lies about God and our circumstances that are such a part of our understanding?

It is absolutely imperative that we begin to exchange our understanding for God's by allowing the "truth" about God and His character to become part of our very existence because the character of God is the only understanding we can look through and see correctly.

Knowledge of the Holy One is understanding.

–Proverbs 9:10

Do you remember God's answer to Moses when he asked, "What is your name?" His answer was "I am who I am." God's character — who He is — is the most important thing about Him. He has to be known for His character because His nature is so vast and complex that no one name can describe Him. God's character — His unchangeableness, His omnipotence, His power, His capacity to love — is more important than anything else.

The problem with our understanding is that we try to figure out

God by looking through the lenses of our circumstances. Are they good? Then God is good. Are they bad? Then God is bad. We get tunnel vision in the midst of a trial and everything we think or know about God is filtered through our circumstances and God's response or lack of response to our situation.

Our experiences of God and life, either good or bad, do not change God. He is the "I am." He is always the same and His love, which is without measure, is always the same. That love, His love, is always flowing toward you. It is active. It is moving, constantly in motion, constantly surrounding you.

Circumstances change. Sometimes they are good, sometimes they're bad and sometimes we can't tell at the moment. But our circumstances have nothing to do with God's character and His love. Our circumstances don't change God. Our pain does not diminish God and His love.

Until we come face to face with the deepest, darkest fact of life without damaging our view of God's character, we do not yet know Him.

— Oswald Chambers

* * *

So what is the answer to difficulty in trusting God? When will your understanding finally change enough to enable you to trust and rest in God when difficulties arise?

We've already established that God led the children of Israel into the wilderness because He wanted to teach them about Himself. The first thing God did after delivering the Israelites from Egypt and getting them started on their journey was to give them instructions. Then He told them to "Fix these words of mine in your hearts and minds." (Deuteronomy 11:18)

If we want to see as God sees, our sight must begin with His words to us — "new understanding" — and we must begin to use it by reading, memorizing and meditating upon it. Everything we learn, all the new perspectives we receive and all the wisdom and maturity that God's Spirit imparts to us on our spiritual journey begins and ends in His Word.

However, the Scriptures on their own will not be enough to change our perspectives about our circumstances until they become our foundation for knowing God. If we are to finally move away from our understanding, we must begin by learning the truth about God. The most accurate portrayal of God and His character is obviously in His Word. It is a mirror image of God.

In the beginning was the Word, and the Word was with God, and the Word was God.

–John 1:1

We need to always remember the eternal purposes behind all things — God wants you to know Him. That knowing begins in His Word to us.

* * *

God and the truth about Him must become important to us if we are going to stop leaning on our own understanding. Interestingly, during our wilderness journey the Word of God often becomes our source of strength and instruction. People have always been able to find comfort and solace from the Word of God, but at no other time is it more evident that Scripture is divinely written than times when we need help. The power of God's Word to comfort, inspire and instruct is wonderfully evident in moments of stress, uncertainty and sorrow. Many times a verse becomes the life preserver we pull tightly around us as waves of trouble threaten to drown us.

Dependence upon God's Word becomes a reality during times of trouble as it cradles our hearts over and over. When we search the Scriptures for words of hope or instruction, the Bible becomes more than just a book of information about God and rules to follow — it becomes our lifeline, the tangible link to God that we desperately need. It becomes His Word to us, His intimate voice telling us about Himself and His love for us, and it becomes a foundation upon which our trust in God can be built.

God's Word brings the comfort for which our souls are longing, the instruction for which our questioning hearts are searching and the knowledge of God our minds need in order to trust Him.

The entrance of your words gives light; it gives understanding to the simple.

–Psalm 119:130 (NKJV)

Knowing the Difference

For who knows what is good for a man in life?

–Ecclesiastes 6:12

Do you know what is good? Have you learned enough to comprehend your own lack of understanding and your need for God's understanding?

In light of what we have learned about our understanding or perceptions, we should be ready to more diligently (desperately) seek to know God. It is His character we must learn to know and depend upon — a life-long process filled with exciting discoveries and new freedom from the curse of unbelief that permeates each of us, coloring our perceptions and darkening our view of God.

New understanding is not the ability to know everything God knows about why things happen. It is knowing God's character enough to enable us to live in joy and peace, dependent upon Him.

Study

What was God's answer to Moses' question, "Who are You?" in Exodus 3:13-14? Look up the following Scriptures and write down the characteristic of God given in each one:

- **Deuteronomy 32:4** ____________________
- **Psalm 36:6** ____________________
- **Joshua 23:14** ____________________
- **Psalm 89:8** ____________________
- **Psalm 9:10** ____________________
- **Psalm 89:1-2** ____________________
- **Psalm 36:5** ____________________
- **Psalm 112:4** ____________________

What part of God's nature or characteristics do you need to know and believe in today? ____________________

Read Psalm 131. Can you do what it describes today?

____

What does Psalm 9:10 say is the foundation for trust in God?

____

What should be your source of hope during difficult days (Psalm 130:5)?

____

Because the truth about God is contained in His Word to us, we must begin to take it in, to read it and to meditate upon it. Read and pray Psalm 119. Underline each Scripture that is an affirmation of the value of God's Word (law, commands, decrees). Put an asterisk by each Scripture that can be used as a prayer. All this week, pray these Scriptures to God. Any time you come to Psalm 119 in the future, make it a prayer and ask God to let His Word become a foundation for your life.

Memorize

I have chosen the way of truth; I have set my heart on your laws.
Psalm 119:30

Prayer of Reflection

Dear Father, I want to know You. I want to trust in who You are: faithful, good, merciful, loving, righteous and kind — so many wonderful qualities. All that is good…You are! Help me to want to learn more about You and Your ways. Place a hunger in my heart for Your Word. Amen.

Reflect

Think about qualities or characteristics of God that have been meaningful to you, and then one you need to know better.

Songs in the Night

"She's in a sulk at God, I think."

My mom was talking about a young woman who was living with her and my dad. The woman had begun her first job a few months prior and had saved up enough money for her first car. She'd only had the car for a few weeks when the engine failed.

Compared to problems many people face, this was minor. But for her, it was demoralizing. It was going to be expensive to fix. She was still paying for the car itself, so it would be some time until she could save enough money to pay for repairs.

Her reaction was to strike out at God. Why had He let it happen? She began to find other things to do when it was time for church. She stopped listening to Christian music, and her Bible lay untouched.

It's always the same, isn't it? Deep down, all of us hold God responsible for the things that happen to us. In response to life's hurts and sorrows we almost instinctively lash out at Him. This is understandable behavior if we have not yet grasped that God can be trusted. When pain comes our way, we take it as a personal affront. The pain is "proof" that God doesn't love us or take care of us. In our feelings of rejection, we lash back in anger, bitterness, hurt and withdrawal.

Whether we admit it or not, the feelings are there and they must be dealt with. The irony is that when we most need God, we often won't come to Him.

* * *

At whatever point our circumstances push our faith in God's love and goodness past the breaking point, it is this aspect of the relationship that is so telling. What do we do next? Is our relationship with God strong enough to withstand our disappointments? Are we willing to come to God even when we feel He has failed us? There is a Scripture in Job that describes the common response:

Men cry out under a load of oppression;
they plead for relief from the arm of the powerful.
But no one says, "Where is God my Maker,
who gives songs in the night?"

–Job 35:10

* * *

We feel many things during the circumstances that try our faith — fear, bewilderment, hurt, anger — but nothing brings more pain to our Father's heart than the conscious or unconscious decision to hold ourselves away from Him. Do we say "Where is God, who gives songs in the night?" or do we turn away?

It is the act of coming to God that is so important in times of distress. In the times when your heart's cry is "unfair," and you are questioning His trustworthiness, it is still necessary to come to Him because until you come, you cannot exchange your understanding for His. It doesn't matter whether you come in anger or questioning, the important thing is to come. Some of Job's words about God were close to blasphemy:

In his great power [God] becomes like clothing to me;
He binds me like the neck of my garment.

–Job 30:18

You turn on me ruthlessly;
with the might of your hand you attack me.

–Job 30:21

Yet others showed beautiful faith in the middle of darkness:

I know that my Redeemer lives,
and that in the end he will stand upon the earth.

–Job 19:25

Job is a good picture of all of us. During difficult days we are often a mixture of faith and despair, trust and bitterness. We know intellectually that we can trust God, but our emotions keep tugging at us and our questioning keeps haunting us, making inroads into our faith.

When we pray during times of difficulty our prayers may be seeking, struggling and questioning God, but that is okay. What really matters is that we actually come to God with our turmoil. Our times of struggling will be useful if we will struggle with God, instead of struggling without Him.

As long as we come to Him with our feelings, we are acknowledging Him. When we nurse our hurt and anger, pulling away from God and refusing to spend time with Him in His word and in prayer, we will never exchange our perspective for His.

There are some who don't outwardly turn away from God. They stoically push aside their feelings and continue facing the trials in their own strength, while attending church and persisting in Bible reading and prayer. But if they never deal with God about their sorrows and questions, they have inwardly withdrawn from Him. God knows what is really in our hearts. He sees under the stoicism to the hurt and bitterness, but He can't help us when we are not honest with Him about our feelings.

God will not be shocked by your words of anger. He knows what you are thinking anyway. It is not the emotions He is concerned with, it is what you decide to do with those feelings of outrage and betrayal. Will you withdraw or will you come to Him?

Whenever we do not pray, we are refusing to allow Him to change our hearts and attitudes so that we can walk in trust. Difficult days can be the times of greatest growth in our relationship with God. It is important that we don't shut Him out or ignore Him in those moments.

God wants us to know Him. He wants a relationship with us. That relationship will only be established in communication with Him. It is in communication — in prayer — that God is again connected with us. It is in prayer that we actively seek God. It is in prayer that we submit ourselves to God, and it is in prayer that His wisdom can be imparted to us.

And, often, it is in the wilderness that prayer is learned.

As we've already emphasized, when things are going well, there is a tendency to forget about our relationship with God or to at least relegate it to the backseat in our drive through life. Then when troubles come, often we spend our time fretting, complaining, talking to everyone we know about our problems and running around trying to change things. We spend endless hours justifying our own actions, trying to figure out what is happening, and countless hours trying to stop the pain. We read self-help books and talk about our problems endlessly.

But if we can learn to bring our struggles, our pain, our unbelief and our anger and pour it all out at His feet, then we will begin to receive help, insight and strength to go on. Even when our hearts are screaming for Him to change things, we still must come to Him. God won't be shocked to hear what we have to say. He already knows! As we pour out our hearts to Him, our hurt at the circumstances, our anger at Him for allowing it, our confusion about what He is doing, our questioning about His hand in the events, our resentment of the people and the circumstances — then God is able, while we have our attention focused on Him, to reveal His heart to us.

God knows what our pain feels like. His concern and sharing of our pain will bring immeasurable comfort to our hearts, bringing a new understanding of God's very nature and allowing us to glimpse another side of an all-powerful, mighty creator God — the side that carries our grief and shares our pain.

Jesus, who came to earth to live as a man, was God identifying with man, feeling His emotions and circumstances so He could forever identify with us in our moments of pain and sorrow.

Surely He has borne our griefs and carried our sorrows.

–Isaiah 53:4 (NKJV)

For we have not a high priest who is unable to sympathize with our weaknesses, but we have one who has been tempted in every way, just as we are.

–Hebrews 4:15

When trials come our way and we go to God for His comfort and assurance, He is there to undergird us. Then, as our needs are met, the principles of prayer learned during times of crisis hopefully will become part of our daily existence, making us more aware of the power of prayer. Our hearts are more open to the need for intercession for others and to the role that prayer plays in our relationship with God.

Prayer during trials becomes the tool that forges the bonds between God and us, making Him real to us, bringing the knowledge that we have of Him from our heads down into our hearts. Prayer is the essence of our relationship to God and there is no other way to learn to know Him. We can listen to sermons and teaching, read countless books about rising above our circumstances and about trusting God. But the knowledge gained from those things cannot make a difference in our emotional response to life and its situations if we do not spend time in God's presence.

It is in God's presence where we exchange our understanding for His. It is in His presence where we pour out our emotions of fear, distrust, hurt and anger, and receive back His ability to find contentment in the middle of a storm, and peace in the midst of crisis.

It is in His presence where the principles we have read in His Word are made a part of us as He reveals to us how they apply to our lives and our situations.

It is in His presence where we begin to release ourselves into His hands and allow Him to direct our lives and bring good into every circumstance.

It is in His presence where we begin to fathom His great love for us. It is in His presence where we become aware of His concern for every detail of our lives.

It is in His presence where we acknowledge God as Lord of our lives and learn that we can trust Him, and it is in His presence where we stop leaning upon our own understanding and begin to lean upon His.

It is God who gives songs in the night, and it is God who is waiting with your song, a new love song to be sung just to you, bringing comfort, assurance, love and intimacy when you finally throw yourself upon your Heavenly Father and have it out with Him.

He cannot make sense of your circumstances or bring comfort when you fail to come. Over and over, His call to you is to come, just come.

Hard circumstances will test you, yes. They'll cause bewilderment and pain, yes. But it is what you do during those circumstances that is so important. Do you withdraw or do you say, "Where is God, my maker, who gives me songs in the night?"

Coming to God

Once you become aware that the main business that you are here for is to know God, most of life's problems fall into place of their own accord.
–J.I. Packer, *Knowing God*

In moments of questioning and hurt we often struggle with our feelings toward God. Our "trust" in His goodness has been shaken and we're not sure we want to come to Him.

Knowing "He is the blessed controller of all things" not only brings comfort, but it can be the catalyst to pain and bitterness when we think about the pain in our lives and know that God could prevent it. That knowledge causes us to accuse Him of not being fair, to question His love and, like Job, to question His integrity. As hurt turns to bitterness, we withdraw from Him.

Have you been guilty of withdrawing from God during difficult times? If you are presently in a time of withdrawal or are struggling with an inability to share your real feelings with God, take the time now to pray and ask for help.

Whether you are reading this during a time of real difficulty or you are just enduring the everyday ups and downs of life, I challenge you to consistently spend time in His presence in daily prayer and devotions. If you don't know God, you cannot trust Him.

Study

Read Psalm 145:18. Where is God when we call on Him?

____

Read Jeremiah 30:21-22. What does God promise to those who decide to approach Him? ______________________________

____

____

What was David's question in Psalm 13:1-2? Have you asked the same thing of God? ______________________________

____

____

Read Psalm 88:14. What was David's accusation? Have you ever accused God in the same way? ______________________________

____

____

Read Matthew 27:46. What similar words did Jesus use?

____

Read Psalm 103:13-14. What is God's attitude toward us?

____

____

____

What is God's call in Jeremiah 31:3? ______________________________

What should be our response (Psalm 27:8)? ______________________

Look up and underline Zephaniah 3:17.

Memorize

But as for me, it is good to be near God. I have made the Sovereign Lord my refuge; I will tell of all your deeds.
Psalm 73:28

Prayer of Response

Dear Heavenly Father, it is difficult to come to You in a real way about what I'm feeling. I'm angry and hurt. It seems easier not to deal with it. I'm not sure where to begin, but I ask for Your help. Forgive me for shutting You out and help me to want to come back into a real relationship with You again. Amen.

Reflect

If you have committed yourself to begin a devotional time, share that commitment with someone else. Keep each other accountable. Ask the Holy Spirit to help you approach your time with God in eager expectation.

New Understanding

My husband and I started our business with enthusiasm. Such high hopes! With God's obvious leading we were able to branch off from an already successful company and begin our own. The business took off and grew rapidly. We quickly took on a partner, opened other locations, hired more employees and…completely over-extended ourselves.

After two years, we were selling over $2 million a year in merchandise, yet we were on the verge of bankruptcy. We sold one location, got rid of the partner by giving him the other branch and began to struggle to stay afloat.

Following months of incredible hardships and stress we went to see the best bankruptcy attorney we could find. We asked for his help in filing Chapter 11, which permits companies to reorganize while keeping creditors at bay until the business is out of trouble. The fee for this service was $15,000, but worth it to save our business. The attorney looked at our accounts, our customer base and our books, and called us in.

"I won't take your money," he said. "There is no way you can pull this out. Save yourself from a nervous breakdown and file bankruptcy."

Disheartened, we thanked him for his advice and came home to seek God's counsel. In the difficult weeks that followed, we kept praying until we both agreed that we would not file bankruptcy until forced into it by creditors. We put the business in God's hands and kept going.

What a testimony it would be if I could tell you that God honored that decision, gave us a miracle and we are now prosperous and happy.

But in reality, that was just the beginning of long and difficult years of struggling and hardship. After several years, we finally came to a point where we could sell the business and break even. Because we were thoroughly weary of it all, we tried very hard to sell. However, God blocked every deal. We couldn't just close the business because we were accountable for service on the equipment that we had sold over the years.

We were forced to go on, but even though we had come to a break-even point financially, we had no capital and no way to borrow money. So things continued the same way: no money to buy product to sell and with no product to sell, no way to get money to buy product to sell — a vicious cycle filling our lives with turmoil and stress.

At any point, God could have stepped in and altered our situation and brought us quickly out of the mess. He did not. During this time, I took over the supply department of our business and experienced firsthand the stress of trying to meet the demands of customers who needed supplies for the equipment we had sold them, creditors who needed money before selling us supplies, employees needing paychecks, and on and on.

During those days, trust and my relationship with God took on very practical terms. It was necessary to pray for money to come in, for supplies to come in on time, for sales, for patience from our customers when they had to wait and for favor and patience from the creditors. I learned that God did not always come through for me in the way I wanted. He didn't always answer my desperate cry for help by changing the circumstances or intervening to get us out of tight spots. Sometimes He didn't send money for payroll on time. Sometimes the supplies we desperately needed didn't come in on time so we could retain the customer. Sometimes the absolutely-vital-to-us employees did quit, and sometimes things were just plain unfair. At one point we had to pay $50,000 in penalties because of errors that other people made on our taxes.

Some circumstances were more difficult to take than others. When things overwhelmed me I would get in my car, go home and rage at God: "You could take care of this. You could have kept this from happening! You could have brought the money in, or saved the deal, or kept the employee. Why didn't You? Where are You, God? Don't You care? I thought I was Your child. I thought You loved me and would take care of me!"

As I cried and directed my anger at God, I always had to come back to a decision. Thankfully, God always helped me to make the right one — the decision to say, "God, I hate all this but You are what is most important to me. I choose to trust in Your love for me anyway!"

In order to survive our circumstances without a nervous breakdown, we had to learn to constantly throw ourselves on God, sometimes like small, frustrated children beating on His chest. But He would always hold us until we quieted in His arms. And even though He wasn't doing things the way we wanted, even though He didn't always deliver us at the last minute, even though He sometimes waited until the thing we dreaded did come upon us, we still had to look to Him and say, "Though the fig tree does not bud and there are no grapes on the vines, though the olive crop fails and the fields produce no food, though there are no sheep in the pen and no cattle in the stalls, yet I will rejoice in the Lord, I will be joyful in God my Savior." (Habakkuk 3:17-18)

That is what learning to trust God is like. It's how our understanding gives way to God's, and it's how we learn He is enough.

I can look back now and see that the times my relationship with God grew the most were not the times of last-minute deliverances, even though God did deliver us many times. It wasn't the times of divine intervention, although we saw that happen too. It was not during the days when we could see God's obvious help and blessing. It grew the most when the very things I dreaded did occur. The money for payroll didn't come in. The long-awaited order didn't arrive in time to save the deal. We did lose the customer, or we did have to pay the tax penalties.

Yet the things I feared, those that caused me the most worry and dread, lost their power over me after I had gone through them without deliverance. Each time, I came to the realization: "Yes, it is bad, but God is still with me and He is enough!" My circumstances didn't change, but I did, and so my relationship with God grew deep and abiding as I learned to put my trust not in what He could or would do for me, but — in Him, just Him.

It is not deliverance from situations that ultimately gives us peace and trust in God. It is God Himself. Each time I decided to say, "Even though you don't deliver me, God, I still want You. I still choose to follow and serve You," my faith and trust in God grew roots deep into my heart. Successive times of adversity then failed to bring the panic and fear of "What would God do?" or "Would He deliver me?". I had grown confident in Him, at rest in His love and secure in my relationship with Him.

You will keep in perfect peace him whose mind is steadfast, because he trusts in you.

–Isaiah 26:3

The hardest part of trusting God is believing in His loving care when harsh circumstances seem to say He's forgotten us, that He couldn't possibly love us or He wouldn't allow…

this pain to continue…

my child to suffer…

my loved one to die…

my bills to be unpaid…

my dreams to never come true.

How can we possibly accept these circumstances as part of His will for us and still believe that His love for us is immeasurable, that His love is constant and continuously flowing? It is difficult to always believe in God's perfect love. At times the circumstances scream louder than our knowledge of His love and they overshadow our slowly growing attempts to lean on His understanding instead of our own.

There will be moments when the darkness of our circumstances seems much more real than the light of His love. It is an unavoidable part of life that every child of God will walk through at some point. But for each of us, the days of despair will grow shorter as we begin to learn to trust God. As we grow in faith, the times of distrust and questioning will lessen.

However, the journey to trust is a battle. There is no other word to describe the days of intense questioning, the days of sorrow as we see our hopes dashed and our prayers go unanswered, and the days of floundering to find some kind of meaning and purpose in what seems so senseless. Trust in God is the only source of peace in a world of changing, senseless circumstances, but it does not come easily; not the kind of faith that is talked about in Hebrews 11: tried, tested, hang-in-there kind of faith — the kind of faith that chooses to keep coming to God in spite of the questioning, the bewilderment and the lack of reasons why.

This kind of faith comes only as a result of a choice, a choice to believe in God and His love for us in spite of what our circumstances say. Over and over we will face that choice. Over and over we will have to choose whether we will look past our "understanding" and choose to believe in God.

It is a choice to pick up the Bible and read what it says about God instead of listening to what our emotions are screaming at us.

It is a choice to ask the Holy Spirit for help in trusting when we really want to rage at the unfairness.

It is a choice to acknowledge God by confronting Him with our pain instead of shutting Him out in bitterness.

It is a choice to continue to ask for help when months of unanswered prayers seem to say it is useless.

It is a choice to believe in what the Word of God says about God and His character.

It is a choice to believe and hold on to the promises in His Word He has given you.

It is a choice to believe He is the blessed controller of all things and He will bring good from every circumstance He allows into your life.

Handling Pain

Jesus said there are times when God cannot lift the darkness from you, but you should trust Him. At times God will appear like an unkind friend, but He is not; He will appear like an unnatural father, but He is not; He will appear like an unjust judge, but He is not. Keep the thought that the mind of God is behind all things strong and growing. Not even the smallest detail of life happens unless God's will is behind it. Therefore, you can rest in perfect confidence in Him.

– Oswald Chambers, ***My Utmost for His Highest***

Whether the catalyst is tragedy, years of unanswered prayers, sickness or any other unresolved problem, we each will come to a place where we must resolve to trust God anyway. It's a place where we decide whether or not we will continue in a relationship with a God who cannot always be understood, cannot be manipulated by our desires or even our pain; a God who seems, at times, to be harsh and unyielding. Are you facing the choice of whether or not you will trust God? How have you been handling the difficult days when it seems God is not listening, not helping and doesn't care about what you are going through?

Study

How is the relationship with God described in Isaiah 63:16 and 1 John 3:1?

____

____

____

Read Matthew 5:45 and Deuteronomy 8:5. What are two reasons we suffer in this life, even as "sons"? ______________________________

____

____

____

Read and meditate on Hebrews 12:1-12. To some, discipline seems like anger or disapproval and they view hardships or trials as a sign of God's disapproval. How does verse 6 answer this? ______________

____

____

____

List some of the statements or instructions from this section of Scripture that will help us exchange our understanding for God's.

____

____

Read Jeremiah 29:11, 1 Corinthians 10:13 and Hebrews 13:5. What does God promise us as an encouragement during difficult times?

____

____

Memorize

"For I know the thoughts that I think toward you," says the Lord, "thoughts of peace and not of evil, to give you a future and a hope."
Jeremiah 29:11 (NKJV)

Prayer of Response

Dear Father, sometimes my relationship with You seems too hard. I just don't know why You do what You do and I'm not always sure I want a close relationship with a God whose ways seem too hard to understand. But today I'm making a choice — a choice to trust You, a choice to believe You are good and a choice to believe in Your love for me and Your desire to bring good into my life. Help me, Lord, to always choose to trust You no matter what comes my way. Amen.

Reflect

1. Think about God's desire for a relationship with you and what that means. Do you desire a close relationship with your Heavenly Father? Even if it means enduring hardship?
2. Think of a time when you were facing difficulties and it seemed God was not helping. What happened? Share your story with others.

Turning Worry into Faith

Jim unlocked the front door of his business and walked quickly to the alarm system to deactivate it, just as he had done a thousand times before. But reaching up toward the pad of numbers to enter the code, his mind suddenly went blank. He knew he had only 90 seconds after unlocking the door to enter his code. If he didn't, the alarm would sound, a signal would go off at the central security office and the police would be notified that there was a break-in.

Jim continued to stare at the numbers, his hand poised to dial in his code, but for some reason, he could not think of the numbers that were as familiar to him as his own name.

How odd, he thought. *I've never forgotten the numbers before.*

Concentrating as hard as he could he tried to recall the code.

4790? No, that wasn't it.

3529? Nope.

Continuing to look at the numbers, Jim found it harder and harder to think because of the realization that the seconds were quickly passing.

6284? No…

He shook his head and glanced down at his watch. This was silly. Why couldn't he remember?

3467…

Giving up, he tried to think of where he had written the code for just an occasion as this. *It must be in the book the security company gave me,* he thought…

"Rrrrrrrrrr!!" The alarm began to sound. Quickly he ran back to his office, threw open a file drawer and frantically began to search for the book.

The phone rang just as he found it. It was the alarm company. He flipped through the pages of the book as he talked to them, trying to explain what had happened. It was hard to talk with the deafening noise of the alarm going off around him. The alarm company was sympathetic in a cautious way, but insistent that they needed to hear the code or the police would soon be on their way.

Finally, Jim found the code, shaking his head as he looked at the familiar numbers. Quickly, he repeated them to the security office before hurrying to the front of the office to deactivate the system and stop the alarm.

* * *

While Jim was telling me about his experience with his alarm system and the frustration he felt as he tried to remember a familiar number, I thought about how often the same thing happens to us when we are confronted with situations that bring turmoil, stress and worry. How often we look at circumstances and, even though we have been through countless situations before in which God has seen us through, we seem to blank out and are unable to bring the truth about God that we know so well into the forefront of our minds and hearts.

Just like in Jim's situation, the panic escalates as we frantically look at our circumstances and wonder how we're going to get through them. With our eyes on the situation, the turmoil of our hearts keeps us from thinking clearly. We can't seem to remember the faithfulness of our God. We forget that "He is the blessed controller of all things" and that He can be trusted in all situations.

All of us will face stressful situations. A phone call, a visit to the doctor, a summons to the boss's office, and immediately we are plunged into a new test of our faith and a new opportunity for fear to replace our trust in God.

I was talking to a close friend recently who had just returned to work after a year's medical leave. When she returned it was to a probationary period and a boss who didn't want her there. Every detail of her work was scrutinized. The pressure to do her best made it hard to work efficiently and quickly.

Day after day, she came home exhausted from the stress. As we discussed her situation I reminded her that God is the blessed controller of all things. She knew that intellectually and yet it was hard to keep her feelings of fear and worry in check. The knowledge didn't seem to be making a difference in her response to the situation. That's exactly the problem for all of us, isn't it? At some point we have to learn how to trust in God in such a way that it will make a difference in us, freeing us from the anxieties and stress that would mar our lives and destroy our peace and trust in God. Every trial we face is meant for our good!

We know that in all things God works for the good of those who love him.

–Romans 8:28

How do we receive the good and how do we get through the difficult days with any measure of serenity? We need to realize we cannot trust God in our own strength. Our need to be able to trust God in a way that makes a difference in our responses to life is one of the primary reasons He promised His Holy Spirit to us. God knew we would need His own Spirit at work in us in order to get through all that life throws at us. If we are to receive the help of the Holy Spirit, we have to turn our eyes away from our circumstances and put them on God by continuing to remember the following principles:

1. Go directly to God. As easy as that sounds, it is often the last thing we think of. The book of 1 Samuel relates a story from David's life that is a perfect example. One day, when he was still living in exile, David and his men returned to the village where they had been living to find the Amalekites had raided the town, burning it and taking everyone captive, including the families of David and his men. The Bible says that David and his men wept aloud until they had no strength left to weep. David was especially distressed because the men turned on him in their anguish, blaming him for the situation, and began to talk of stoning him.

Then the narrative goes on to say: "But David found strength in the Lord his God." (1 Samuel 30:6)

I like how the King James version says it: "But David encouraged himself in the Lord his God."

What a wonderful example for us in our days of stress and times of trial! Several things need to happen as we come to God, however. When we come to Him, it is important that we stay as long as it takes to receive help. Often, we simply pour out our litany of worries and then walk away. It isn't enough just to rehearse the problem over and over with God. We must also commit ourselves and the problem to Him. It is only then that we can receive new faith and new strength to keep going and new assurance of His love and care.

David's psalms are a beautiful example of the way to pray during problems. David was very honest in sharing his feelings with God: betrayal, hurt, anger, questioning and confusion. Yet he always came to a point of releasing those feelings and stating words of faith, such as something about God and His character, words of assurance that God had heard him or words of praise and thanksgiving for past kindnesses. These kinds of words reflect an attitude of heart that is vital if we are to overcome worry and develop our trust in God.

2. Learn to know when you are most vulnerable to worry. Most people are more fearful at night. Learn how to circumvent the fearful thoughts by guarding your mind. You can do this with quick prayers for help:

"Holy Spirit, I ask for Your peace in my mind and heart right now."

"Dear Jesus, put a guard around my thoughts. Help me not to listen to fearful thoughts."

"God, I believe You are the blessed controller of all things."

Learn to argue against words of fear, blame, discouragement and thoughts that question His goodness and trustworthiness. Worrisome thoughts are not God's will for your life, so that kind of thinking is never from God. He will always want to help you return to an attitude of peace, trust and rest.

3. During difficult times, when your trust is stretched to its limits, you may have to ask for help often during the day. When problems seem insurmountable and troubling thoughts assault you, ask for help right then. This turns trials into wonderful "learning to lean" times as we learn to lean hard upon God all day long for help in getting through the day. These kinds of situations enable us to grow close to God very quickly if we keep calling out to Him moment by moment.

4. Use the energy of worry and transform it into prayer. The most positive thing you can do in the middle of a problem is to use the anxiety to drive you to prayer. Crying out to God for help, deliverance and understanding is what God wants you to do and is the first and best response when circumstances threaten your peace and trust in Him.

God is genuinely moved by our tears and our concerns. We need not hold back our emotions as we pray.

5. Some circumstances we find ourselves in are actually God's catalyst or way of calling us into intercession. God's purpose for allowing some distressing situations into your life may be so you will pray diligently for His will to be done in that situation or in someone's life. It is important to remember when other people are involved in a way that is hurtful to us to ask God to help us pray with His compassion and without judgment on our part.

6. As you come to God in prayer, ask Him to give you discernment to know if spiritual warfare prayer is needed. Ephesians 6:10-18 reminds us that we are opposed by spiritual forces of darkness and Satan's "fiery darts." We are told that we wrestle with rulers and powers of the dark world and we are instructed to stand against them. We are instructed to be clothed in the full armor of God and to use the Word of God as an offensive weapon.

7. Devour the Word of God. Read Psalms, meditate on faith-building Scriptures and memorize Scriptures that apply to your situation. The Word of God changes us, uplifts us and empowers us as it brings faith and truth into our situations.

The Word of God will expose the fear and distortions that cause us to forget about God's care and love. It will remind us of who God is.

I am completely discouraged —
I lie in the dust.
Revive me by your Word.

–Psalm 119:25 (LB)

8. Remember God's past faithfulness. Rehearse the many times God has helped you in the past. See Psalms 143:1-5.

9. Keep an attitude of praise. The Word of God commands us to praise Him. Praising God will often be the key to unlocking a supernatural attitude of trust in the middle of distressful problems. The story of Jehoshaphat in 2 Chronicles 18 is a wonderful example of this principle in action.

Don't worry if your praise begins just as dry words. Keep saying them; quote Scripture about God's character or sing praise songs. Make up your own songs to Scriptures and sing them. Eventually, your feelings will come into line with the truths you are repeating.

10. Pray daily. It is imperative when you are walking through a trial that you remember to exchange your understanding for God's on a daily basis. As days turn into weeks and weeks into months and you still struggle with an ongoing problem, there will be new battles to fight as you try to maintain trust. You will fight some battles over and over again as despair threatens to rob you of your peace and trust in God, and impatience creeps in to threaten your hard-won faith. It will be necessary to come back to God again and again with new cries for help to keep trusting in the face of unanswered prayer.

Fighting Fear

There are days when you wake up with the circumstances staring you in the face. It will be a struggle to regain the peace God has given you over and over. But it is worth the effort. Don't just allow your fears to take control. Immediately cry out for help, then begin to fight against despair, worry and unbelief with the Word of God. Look up Scriptures that contradict the worry thoughts. It can be a promise He has given you, a statement of belief in His control of circumstances, a description of His character or a reminder of His love for you. Read or quote the Scriptures out loud to God, reaffirming your belief in those words.

A simple prayer will always provide the help of the Holy Spirit:

"Father, in Jesus' name, I ask You to bring my emotions back into line with Your will for me. I submit my emotions to the Lordship of Jesus."

"Father, bring my thoughts into line with Your will for me."

Some days may take more discipline as you fight against fears with Scripture and pray more than once for His thoughts instead of your own. 2 Corinthians 10:5 instructs us to take our thoughts captive and make them obedient to Christ. In other words, our thoughts should be reflections of Christ — or truth, based on God's Word. When we fight worry thoughts with truth from God's Word, we are doing what this Scripture instructs us to do. God always has victory for you. He provided the Holy Spirit, your helper, to enable you to be victorious. He wants you to walk in peace.

Study

What words in 1 Timothy 6:12 describe what we are doing when we exercise the principles in this chapter? ____________________

____

____

What does Psalm 62:8 say is part of trusting in God at all times?

____

What instruction does Psalm 103:2 give us? ____________________

____

What does 1 Corinthians 2:16 say about our minds?

____

____

Now look up Philippians 2:5. What truth does this Scripture reveal?

____

____

Memorize

We demolish arguments and every pretension that sets itself up against the knowledge of God, and we take captive every thought to make it obedient to Christ.
2 Corinthians 10:5

Prayer of Response

Dear heavenly Father, I know sometimes I fail miserably in trusting You because I wallow too long in fear. Forgive me and help me to more quickly come and ask for help in days of stress and uncertainty. Help me to continue in the process of exchanging my understanding for Yours. I want my thoughts to be a reflection of Christ's thoughts and His trust in You. Amen.

Reflect

What kinds of problems cause you to forget that God is good and faithful?

Part Three

In All Your Ways Acknowledge Him

Off the Edge

We taught our children to swim at a very early age, and although our son Matthew took to the water like a little duck, Jula was more hesitant. Each step in the process of getting her "waterproofed" seemed to be a major production, such as the day she learned to jump into the water. I can still picture her standing on the edge of the pool trying to get the courage to jump in…

Nervously, she hopped from one foot to the other, her blond pigtails bouncing up and down as she would start to jump, then stop herself, over and over again.

Standing in the water, I held out my arms and tried to coax her. "Come on, Jula, jump! I'll catch you!"

She looked over at her brother, confidently jumping in all by himself, and then back at me standing in the water.

"Come on, honey!"

The expression on her face was easy to read as she wavered back and forth: *Do I really want to do this? It looks like fun, but will she catch me? Will I go under?* Her instinctive fears of the unknown struggled with her desire to please me and do what her brother was doing.

"You can do it!" I urged.

She crouched down again, her eyes growing big as she determined to really do it this time. She moved to jump and then tried to stop herself, but it was too late. Over the side she came, arms flailing and legs kicking. As I reached out and caught her, she grabbed me and held on tight.

"See? Wasn't that fun?" I asked. She laughed nervously and looked over to see if her brother had been watching. Gently, I bobbed up and down in the water with her and then walked around for a moment.

Then I sat her back up on the side of the pool and said, "Let's do it again." Her face fell and she started squirming and looking around. She didn't cry or say anything, but her reluctant expression still spoke volumes: *What? Wasn't once enough?*

But when she glanced over at Matthew, happily jumping in the water and crawling out to do it all over again, her expression changed again and she moved a second time to the edge. She started hopping up and down, just like before, trying to work up her courage. She was probably still thinking, *Okay, so she caught me once, but will she catch me again?*

She struggled with it while I persuaded, "Come on, Jula. I'm right here. It was fun, wasn't it?"

Finally, with one last peek at Matthew, another look of determination came across her face. She leaned forward and hurled herself into the water and into my waiting arms. Soon she was climbing out on her own and running over to the side to jump into my arms over and over, laughing excitedly and hugging me each time I caught her.

It's scary, isn't it, to throw ourselves into the unknown, to place our lives into another's care — to "trust" someone? We instinctively hold back all or part of ourselves in those kinds of situations.

The Hebrew root word for "trust" suggests "to fling oneself off a precipice." What a great word picture for our relationship with God! At times it really does seems like we are flinging ourselves into the unknown, believing in a God who can't be seen or heard, choosing to embrace a belief that says God is good in spite of all the evil we see around us.

If we have decided to trust God, that belief demands a response; a "leap off the precipice" as we begin to "live" as someone who really trusts God. If I believe that my heavenly Father is concerned about my life, will I live in a way that reflects my belief that He is the blessed controller of all things by "acknowledging Him in all things"?

Acknowledging God is a way of life that incorporates two distinct actions on our part — first, the need to acknowledge God by submitting to Him, and second, the need to acknowledge God by accepting everything that comes into our lives as allowed by God:

1. *Submission/obedience*

This is simply a matter of who is going to be in control. Wrapped up in trusting God is the willingness to give Him control of our lives. This may not seem difficult when things are going the way "we" like. But often, when we're grappling with harsh circumstances, it is hard to let God work things out in His way and in His time.

There will be some situations we face where we will not get our way. There will be times when we face the choice whether we will do things our way or God's way. It can be difficult when God's way doesn't seem like it will get us out of the painful situations we're in; when it seems God's way couldn't possibly bring us happiness. However, it should be fairly obvious that if we want God to bring good out of our circumstances, we are also going to have to submit to His ways.

Sometimes the good that God brings will at first run counter to the "results" or "good" that we might want to come from our situation. This goes back to our lack of understanding again. Our strong self life is going to struggle against some of the "good" that God may want to bring about in situations such as: repentance, forgiving those who have hurt us, putting others before ourselves, giving up our "rights" to what we want and giving up our "right" to bitterness, self pity and anger over the way we've been treated.

Submission to God's will is "acknowledging Him" in all our ways. It is acknowledging His right in our lives. It is making Him not only our Savior and helper, but our Lord, and it is believing that He knows, better than us, what is best for us.

2. *Acceptance*

Acknowledging God in all our ways also means we must accept all things that come our way as allowed by God. This is imperative if we are to ever receive His good from some of the difficult situations we may face. Nothing happens to a Christian because God wasn't looking or because God couldn't stop it from happening. In every thing that comes our way, we must first come into an attitude of acceptance that God allowed it into our lives and He wants to bring good.

The need for "acceptance" may seem fairly obvious when dealing with tragedies and irreversible circumstances, but what about all of the other kinds of situations that come our way: sickness, unfair treatment, relationship problems, disappointments, unfulfilled goals, etc. Sometimes it is harder for us to "accept" those kinds of situations as being allowed by God for our good. Yet when we don't acknowledge God's sovereignty in these kinds of circumstances we are thwarting God's ability to bring good from them. We keep God from being able to use our circumstances to deal with the character flaws that are a part of each one of us, and we keep Him from being able to mature us spiritually. Often, we find ourselves making the same mistakes and going through the same problems over and over again.

Acceptance does not mean God will not change our circumstances. It doesn't mean we shouldn't pray for deliverance and ask for help. It also doesn't mean there won't be actions we will need to take in times of difficulty. It simply means we must acknowledge God first and then move toward finding His purpose and His plan for good.

God can do many things in our lives through any trial we may face. When He doesn't immediately change our circumstances, He may want to:

- begin to bring the fruit of the Spirit into our lives in ever-increasing measure (James 1:2).
- move us along in our maturity level and teach us to trust Him in spite of difficulties.
- deal with our willfulness and reveal wrong motives and wrong reactions.
- point out the self-will, pride, self pity or desire to please that may be behind the trouble we are in. He may want to reveal the self-centeredness that causes so many of our problems, especially relational ones.
- help us to deal with the woundedness from our past that continues to affect our life and our relationship with Him.
- teach us the principles of spiritual warfare (how to stand against Satan's attacks, in the authority given us by Christ) and how to persevere in prayer as we seek for change in our circumstances.
- loosen the grip the world has on us with its all-consuming pleasures, sorrows and ambitions.

Just one or all of the above may be what God has in mind when He allows a hurtful situation to come our way or to continue. However, the good that God wants to bring starts with an attitude of trust and acceptance. It starts with a decision to do things God's way, and a decision to acknowledge Him in all our ways.

Certainly, God is a God of comfort. When troubles come, He is most desirous of being a comfort and solace to us. He wants to draw us close and allow us to lean hard upon Him during difficulties, grief and pain. But there will also be times when we draw close to God during times of hurt and, as we look into His face, we must be willing to receive not only His love and comfort, but also His loving correction, His patient instruction, His wise counsel and His piercing insight into our motives and deepest feelings.

When we begin to acknowledge God in all our ways, He will be able to impart to us His knowledge, His understanding, His character and His grace, so we can begin to walk in trust.

Let us acknowledge the Lord.
Let us press on to acknowledge Him.

–Hosea 6:3

Giving Up Control

There comes a time for all of us when God deals with our propensity to try to solve our own problems and our attempts to bring about the results we want in the circumstances in which we find ourselves. Some are more challenged than others with this matter of "wanting our own way," but even those easy-going types will eventually come to a place where God puts a finger on the areas over which they insist on retaining control. There will be times of crisis for each of us; times when we will reach a crossroads where we will struggle with the decision of whether to go God's way or our own. We will face times when we have to choose to acknowledge His right in our lives in all things.

We are all desperately trying to make ourselves happy using the tools we think are best (our desires, our abilities), not realizing that our flawed personalities, our sin natures and our painful pasts all work together to trip us up over and over again. When we have not yet learned to submit our lives completely to God, we will continue to make mistake after mistake, wrong choice after wrong choice, and face failure after failure. We must eventually give up our faith in ourselves and our abilities to work things out the way we want. This is where "trust in God" becomes active. This crossroads is when we see whether we really do believe God is "the blessed controller of all things."

Study

Read Jeremiah 10:23. What does this Scripture say about life? ______________________________

Read Jeremiah 17:10. What is the problem with our ways?

____

____

Read Jeremiah 17:5-8. Contrast the cursed man in verses 5 and 6 with the blessed man in verses 7 and 8. What is the cursed man's problem?

____

____

Isaiah 50:10-11 gives instruction to people who are walking through difficult times. What does verse 11 tell people who want to solve the problem of darkness in their own way? ______________________________

____

____

What torches do you use to light your own way? ____________________

____

____

In what good things (lit torches are not inherently bad!) do you put your trust?

____

____

Memorize

Commit your way to the Lord; trust in him.
Psalm 37:5

Prayer of Response

Dear Father, I have been guilty of trying to "light my own path" by trusting in myself instead of You. I acknowledge Your right in my life in all things. And Father, even as I make a new commitment today, I know this will have to be lived out in the details, both large and small, of my life. I ask for Your help. I want to have a submitted heart. Jesus, help me to be like You…to submit as You did in all things.

Reflect

Share with another person the areas in which you find it easier to trust in yourself than in God. Pray for one another.

Submission

Several years ago I was talking with a friend who was dating a non-Christian. She and the man were considering marriage even though she knew she should only marry a believer. "I don't want to read my Bible too much or pray too much," my friend explained about her situation, "because I don't want to hear what God has to say."

I hardly knew how to respond. She had been a Christian since she was a young girl. She was raised in a Christian home, and knew God and His commands. She was continuing to go to church and live as a Christian in all other areas, yet she was maintaining this "relationship" with God while at the same time she was in the middle of rebellion against what she knew to be His will.

How often do we want God in our life but on our own terms? How many of us have sections of our lives in which we shut God out? We live as Christians — praying, attending church, perhaps even studying the Bible — yet all the while we ignore principles that don't fit our choices. We tell God we love Him, we talk to Him and we read the Bible and go to church. Yet we refuse to submit to His lordship. Many times it isn't because we want to blatantly do something against God's commandments. Often it is simply because we want to be left alone to serve God the way we want.

We don't want to totally rebel. Oh, no! Most of us are afraid of that. We know we need God, and we want Him in our life, but our carnal nature keeps us from casting ourselves upon Him totally in submission. So we ignore God's dealing in our lives, making the relationship with Him a distant one because closeness would carry with it too much pressure to conform to His will.

We're just not sure we can trust Him with "all" of our lives. We're convinced we wouldn't like what He requires of us. We're sure that in "this" area we know best, or in "this" circumstance our way is the only way we'll be happy. We're positive that we can't do all He wants us to do.

I know people who have lived for years in "mini-rebellion" against God. They attend church (some even pastor churches), they follow the basic tenets of God's Word and they seek God for help during troublesome times, but they continue to keep "no trespassing" signs on parts of their lives. To keep those signs there, they cannot walk closely with God in intimate fellowship.

The areas in which people refuse to submit vary greatly from person to person. For some it's as basic as their refusal to tithe. For others, it is a refusal to obey God's call to some kind of ministry. For some, it is a denial of their need to change when God deals with character traits, or refusing to give up lifestyles or habits that are displeasing to God. It may be choosing to keep their pet sins: anger, lust, self pity, criticism, etc.

Others think their circumstances are "different." They can't believe the rules and instructions in God's Word apply to their situations. For example: "God wouldn't want me to stay with a husband [or wife] I don't love…how could He bring good from that?"

With many it is simply an unwillingness to come any closer in a relationship with God. It is a constant decision to keep God at arms length, knowing that close interaction will mean the need to acknowledge Him in all our ways. Our carnal natures convince us that it would be the end of life the way we're used to, the way we "want" it, with ourselves still retaining control.

People who make the decision to deny God's right in their lives, whether they are as up front about it as my friend was or whether it is a matter they never really face, all must become aware that they cannot live a life of trust and rest in God when they are saying "hands off" to Him. They must understand that God cannot work for good in everything in their lives because they are refusing to acknowledge Him in all their ways by obeying Him.

Over a two-year period, the Israelites watched God perform miracle after miracle on their behalves. He led them with a cloud by day and fire at night. He miraculously gave them food to eat and water to drink. His visible presence rested upon the tabernacle. He spoke to them with an audible voice. There was instant deliverance, instant justice and instant instruction. But none of it was enough when it came time for them to take Canaan. Fearful and rebellious, they chose to believe a scary report about giants even though God had literally moved megatons of water apart to let them escape Pharaoh's army just a few years before. Their choice forced them to repeat their journey through the wilderness over and over.

How many trips around Mt. Sinai have you made lately? Are you still walking around it? Do you know why yet? Is there a situation in your life you are dealing with right now and you just can't surrender all of it to God?

Or perhaps you're in the middle of a problem and God hasn't "delivered" you in the way you want and you're looking at "giants" that seem insurmountable. You've decided to take care of it yourself.

When we look at our problem or our sorrow and say, "This is bad and I cannot stand it" or "This is bad and I should not have to put up with it," the next step may be to give up on God and go back to what we really trust in: ourselves.

From that point on we begin to make decisions and do whatever we can to make things better for ourselves:

sometimes with seemingly innocent pursuits of self-fulfillment;

sometimes with a quiet inner withdrawal from intimate fellowship;

sometimes with what seems on the surface to be good attempts at problem solving;

sometimes with blatant leaps of disobedience and disregard for God's laws.

We jump into affairs and out of marriages. We go back to harmful lifestyles. We give up on our fight against the immoral habits still lingering from our youth. We justify our actions with all kinds of smoke screens and words of justification. We find excuses to not attend church because we know we will be confronted with our bitterness toward God. Our Bibles are left unopened, and our prayers become rote.

When we've decided God has failed us and we can't trust Him, we pull away from any real intimacy with Him. We may continue Christian activities if that is the lifestyle we're used to, but our choices reflect what we really think about God. We may never really admit that we've given up trusting God and that we've decided He can't be trusted to fix our problems. We may never say He is not enough to bring us peace and contentment in the middle of our pain and grief, but our actions says God has failed us and we must find our own way.

The choice is ours. Do we acknowledge God by submitting to Him completely, believing He will work good in our circumstances? Or do we choose to believe that we hold the key to our own happiness?

* * *

In order to enter into Canaan and receive the promise of God's abundant life, the Israelites had to believe that God was leading them and that He would protect them and bring good into their lives. When the time came to cross Jordan, they were called on to "act" on their faith by obeying God's word to them. They had learned to know Him in the wilderness. They had seen over and over that He was faithful and that He would care for them, but the Israelites failed to submit to God in trust. Their failure condemned them to 40 more years in the wilderness.

Our unwillingness to act upon our trust in God by our submission to Him will condemn us to the wilderness also. It will condemn us to a life of mediocrity and sorrow as we wander through the same problems, the same mistakes and the same patterns year after year. We will never be able to enter into the fullness of God and receive all that He can give us until we are willing to give our whole life into His hands in obedient submission, believing in Him and acknowledging Him in all things.

If we believe that nothing touches us unless God allows it, and if we believe He will bring good from all that touches our lives, and if we have decided we will trust God, then those beliefs demand a response.

If you love me, you will obey what I command.

–John 14:15

The last verse of the hymn *Trust and Obey* describes it:

> ***But we never can prove the delights of His love***
> ***until all on the altar we lay;***
> ***But the favor He shows and the joy He bestows***
> ***are for them who will trust and obey.***

Trust and obedience go hand in hand. That is why "In all your ways acknowledge Him" follows "Trust in the Lord with all your heart."

(Proverbs 3:5-6) When we refuse to acknowledge God in everything, we can never really trust Him because we are struggling with Him. We are pulling away in this area or that. We are demanding our way or we are questioning His ability to bring good out of the circumstances of our lives. In this struggle, we cannot be assured of God's hand upon our lives for good because God will never overstep our will. God often has to wait, allowing the consequences of our own willful actions and attitudes into our lives, until we are ready to submit and acknowledge Him in all.

The need for submission covers every part of our lives. It affects many kinds of things: the choices we make, the problems we face, the hurts that come our way and the sinfulness that must be confronted. It includes our past, our daily life, our need for godliness, and all that concerns us.

Trust in God is a wonderful foundation for our lives but trusting God will only come about fully as we learn to submit to Him. These two aspects of our lives — trust and obey — create a spiral affect. As we trust God, we are more willing to submit to Him. As we submit to Him, we learn that we can trust Him.

Walking in Submission

When I am not convinced that God is good, I will quietly — but with tight-lipped resolve — take over responsibility for my own well-being.

– Dr. Larry Crabb, *Finding God*

Larry Crabb describes the attitude behind our refusal to walk in complete submission and obedience with God. We are so often convinced that we know what is best — what will make us happy — and that belief causes us to take actions that often run counter to God's plans, desires and will for us. If you are struggling now with matters that are tempting you to walk in disobedience, it is time to acknowledge the root of it and ask for help.

Study

What do the following Scriptures say about loving God? John 14:15:

____

John 14:21: ______________________________

What does God desire from us that surpasses even our thanksgiving? (Hosea 6:6) ______________________________

Read Isaiah 28:9-13. What is the final result for those who refuse to listen and obey? ______________________________

"Unbelief is the root of all sin." Do you believe this is true?

____

Look up Genesis 3:1-6 and consider the first sin. What did Eve really believe about God? ______________________________

Did she believe He was good and that all He said was good for her?

____

What attitude did she have that is mirrored in us? ______________

____

Memorize

Whoever has my commands and obeys them, he is the one who loves me. He who loves me will be loved by my Father, and I too will love him and show myself to him.
John 14:21

Prayer of Response

Lord, You know I am a person who prefers to solve my own problems. I ask for forgiveness for the many times I have taken matters into my own hands and tried to work things out in my own way and time. Help me to become childlike and patient in faith, trusting in Your goodness and ability to care for me so that I will submit to Your directions, Your timing and Your solutions to my problems. Holy Spirit, I ask for Your help in staying submitted, no matter what the circumstances of my life. Amen.

Reflect

Evaluate an experience from your life in which you decided you knew better than God what was best for you.

Shadows

Our new kitten, Pepper, loves to play. She chases her tail and lies in ambush waiting to attack our feet when we walk by. She runs into paper bags and skids across the kitchen floor, shreds every piece of paper that finds its way to the carpet, climbs my drapes if I don't watch her and generally makes a nuisance of herself.

One morning, I watched her playing by the picture window in the family room. Sunlight was streaming in, drawing her toward the warmth. She was chasing a ball back and forth when suddenly she saw her shadow. Immediately, she began to bristle. Then, with fur on end, she ran at it as fast as she could. She chased it across the room until, all of a sudden, she slammed into the wall. I had to laugh at the puzzled look on her face when she turned around.

She walked back toward the window and then, when she turned just a little, there it was again! She ran and jumped, trying to bat it with her paws, following it until she hit the wall again!!

She got up and looked over at me as if to say, "What's the deal?"

She saw it again, but this time she followed it slowly until finally giving up in frustration.

I smiled as I watched her, thinking how often we humans do the same thing. We chase after problems in our lives, trying to defeat them and get rid of the curse that seems to be following us. We rebuke Satan, we pray for the people who are hurting us that they will see their wrong, we moan about the unfairness of our situations and we continue to hit the walls we have erected around our understanding. Finally, we give up. We decide to ignore it, more sure than ever that God is not in control, or that He just doesn't care.

We never seem to grasp that what we're chasing, what we're struggling with, is our own shadow. We're convinced we're in the mess we're in because of other people, bad luck and circumstances beyond God's control. We struggle with anger, pain, disillusionment and bitterness, never once acknowledging God enough to allow Him to show us that the real source of the problem is us.

We never see that the long shadow of pain has been cast by our own lives; that the problems we're chasing are caused by our own self-centeredness, pride or rebellion, and the deeply-rooted scars that plague our lives and color our perceptions. Our own immaturity continues to catch us up in cycles of defeat. Countless people are walking around with bruises and scars from bumping into walls because they have been chasing shadows instead of acknowledging God.

When we can look back at situations we have faced and we cannot see any good that God has brought to our spiritual life...

When incidents or relationships continue to carry hurt...

When we seem to get caught in the same negative kinds of circumstances over and over again...

When we can't get past the bitterness when memories are stirred...

...then perhaps we're chasing shadows by trusting in ourselves instead of acknowledging God by submitting all of our lives to Him and accepting all of our circumstances as allowed by Him for our good. Of course it takes time to recover from difficult situations, and it takes time to learn from our circumstances, but shouldn't we eventually come to wholeness and maturity? If we believe in God's Word, if we believe that He can be trusted in everything, then the answer is yes.

Unfortunately, when we refuse to submit to God in every circumstance, those vehicles that God allowed into our lives to bring us to a higher plane instead crash at the bottom of the mountain, trapping us inside. There we stay, unable to fully trust God as our relationship with Him continues to be stifled by our refusal to acknowledge Him in all our ways. For some people, it is easier to acknowledge God in the tragedies or life-changing events — losing a loved one, a horrible accident — than it is when they are faced with financial reverses, unfair treatment or problems in their relationships with others. They can lift their faces to God in admirable acceptance of His sovereignty during tremendous hardship, but when they face misunderstandings, lost opportunities, or unfulfilled desires, they can't see that God could be part of it. That blindness inhibits God from using their circumstances to bring good into their lives.

***

Jerry ministered for God most of his adult life, pastoring churches, studying God's Word and teaching principles of truth. He labored diligently year after year. Although he no longer pastors, he continues to teach whenever he has the opportunity, sharing from his vast knowledge of God's Word.

I talked to a mutual friend a few months ago and asked about Jerry, "Is he still attending the same church?"

"No," my friend answered. "He left there last year. He got upset when they didn't ask him to speak one Sunday when the minister was out of town."

I wasn't surprised to hear that. It fit the pattern that had become his life during the last few years. Slights, real or imagined, continued to "hurt" him as he wandered from town to town, church to church, looking for a place to use his talents. The pattern had been set when he was still a young pastor, as he endured many of the problems ministers face with dissatisfied parishioners and church boards who perhaps didn't share his vision or perspective.

His response to the problems had become the pattern for his life: instant denial that any of the problems might be his fault, laborious justification of himself and his actions, continued harboring of feelings of mistreatment and years of seeing injury and insult where often there was none.

It bothered me that a man with his knowledge of God's Word and sincere commitment to God could be so blind to his own need for insight, help and healing in certain areas of his life. What had set him up for this kind of pattern? Was it his childhood? Was it too much pride or was it a problem with self-pity? Was it the accumulation of too many years of pain?

I didn't know, but inwardly I grieved for him: "God, it shouldn't be this way for one of Your children. Especially one who has served You so faithfully for so many years." As I sought understanding, I realized that no one is exempt from God's principles. We're not exempt from His commands for righteousness, and we are not exempt from His commands to trust Him and to acknowledge Him in all our ways.

All of us, even those devoted to God's Word and His work, have blind spots to our own need for inner change. Sometimes whole chunks of our "own understanding" remain in the way, and it may be the harsh or seemingly unfair circumstance that God wants to use to break down our understanding so His light can shine upon our inner self.

Hard circumstances have a way of either bringing beauty to our lives or further molding us into a response pattern of denial, self-pity, self-will, justification, bitterness and blame. It is amazing how set the pattern can become in some people's lives, until it is a continuing cycle becoming ever more prominent in the situations they continue to face. We build higher and higher walls around us, further reinforcing the behavior and response patterns in which we are caught. We continue to say, "God would never want this to happen to me!" "This is unfair!" "They're to blame!" "This is not my fault!" Our refusal to acknowledge God is a refusal to submit to His piercing insight and His quest to teach us, to correct us and to bring maturity and healing to our lives.

There are times when we face tremendous hardships and hurts that are not of our own making. Although God did not cause them, He certainly wants to use them in our lives. There are also times when we do cause our own problems, but we may never realize it if we fail to come to God in acknowledgment.

Then there are the times when the situations we face are because it is time for us to begin to mature spiritually. It isn't that God can't protect us from adverse circumstances or other people's wills, but often God chooses to allow those circumstances and those people into our lives that will put pressure upon those areas that need growth.

Our reactions to situations are not surprising. Each of us faces difficulties blinded by our own unique understanding, personality, sinfulness and background. In all of us there are root problems of sin and distortion that God wants to reveal, cleanse, heal and give us victory over.

In all of us there is a need for maturity, a need for spiritual muscle and faith to be built; in all of us there are godly principles that God wants to impart. In all of us there is a need to receive "His understanding." But He can do none of these things in our lives when we refuse to acknowledge Him in all our ways.

God doesn't waste anything! When we acknowledge God by submitting to Him even in the tumultuous days, He can use the turmoil to help us grow in knowledge of Him. Any circumstance that comes into our lives, God can use in a multitude of ways if we will acknowledge Him in it. This is much easier to do when we can see what God is doing, or when we recognize our need for growth. But often when difficulties come, we would rather rebuke the problems, claim victory over troubles and have our circumstances changed immediately.

It can be painful to acknowledge God when it means coming face to face with our own sinfulness. It can be traumatic to deal with hurts from our past. It's hard to come to grips with our need to change.

We so want to point outward when we are unhappy: to the other person, to the unfair treatment, to the unfulfilled desires or unmet needs. Yet, all the while God wants us to acknowledge Him and His part in our circumstances so that we will begin to open ourselves up to His dealings in our lives. When we finally begin to believe God really loves us and wants to do good in every circumstance, that belief demands a response in times of trial. Will we accept it as allowed by God and submit to Him in it? The problem comes, however, when we see only some of our circumstances as allowed by God for our good and not others.

It is amazing how blind we can be in certain situations, especially in the area of relational problems. We are so aware of other's wrongdoing, so busy pointing a finger, that it never occurs to us to stop and acknowledge that God allowed this circumstance into our lives for our good and our growth.

In any hardship we face, when God does not immediately change our situations, it is time to acknowledge Him by accepting that the circumstances are being allowed by God for our good. Then we need to acknowledge Him by totally submitting ourselves to Him and allowing Him to show us what He wants to do during and through our circumstances.

When times are good, be happy;
But when times are bad, consider:
God has made the one
as well as the other.

–Ecclesiastes 7:14

Admit It

In what "vehicle" have you become trapped because you haven't learned to acknowledge God in all your ways? Are you ready to look at the areas in your life that seem to be a pattern for you? Do you continually go through the same kinds of problems and yet have not seen anything God may be trying to teach you in allowing them to happen over and over? Have you refused to look closely at yourself in relation to your problems to see if God is trying to reveal something to you or bring maturity in a new area?

Perhaps the problems are not necessarily related but just seem to cover a wide continuing spectrum of hardship. One of the first areas you should ask God to show you lies in the realm of self pity, the "Why do I have to go through this?" or "I did nothing to deserve this" attitude. This is often a subtle problem that requires the light of the Holy Spirit for it to be revealed to us in all of its glaring ugliness.

This problem is even harder to recognize and admit when we've been wronged by other people, but it still comes under the heading of "I shouldn't be treated this way." Until our propensities for self pity are acknowledged and repented for, we cannot move on to receive God's good.

Whatever God may be trying to show you, whatever growth He may be trying to bring, you need to open up yourself and be willing to be changed. Offer a prayer of acceptance for the problems you are now in and ask God to use them to do whatever He wants in your life.

Study

Use the following Scriptures to make a list of the benefits of affliction:

Deuteronomy 8:2

Daniel 4:25

Psalm 119:71

Hebrews 5:8

James 1:2-3

1 Corinthians 1:3-5

2 Corinthians 1:8

2 Corinthians 2:3-6

Romans 5:3-5

1 Peter 1:6-8

What did the author of Psalm 119 learn about God through afflictions? (See vv. 67-68) ______________________________

____

What incidents in Israel's history are an example of God's response to complaining and self pity? (see Numbers 11:1-4,10, 31-34)

____

Read 1 Corinthians 10:12. What is one tendency that sets us up for self-pity? ____

Read Galatians 5:19-21. Under which sin of the flesh would self-pity belong? (Hint: Who is in the center of our lives when we are feeling sorry for ourselves or who is our "idol?") ______________________________

____

Memorize

For our light affliction, which is but for a moment, is working for us a far more exceeding and eternal weight of glory.
2 Corinthians 4:17

Prayer of Response

Dear Father, forgive me for the times I have been guilty of the sin of self-pity. If this is a root problem in my life, I ask You to show it to me in all its glaring sin and help me come to true and lasting repentance over it. I want to be set free of all its deadly tentacles that have wrapped themselves in and around me, cutting off the flow of trust in You. Lord, I want You to be at the center of my life. Forgive me for putting myself there. Jesus, I look to You for help and deliverance. Thank You for dying on the cross so that I can be free of this sin. Amen.

Reflect

What promises do we need to remember when our faith is being tried? (Jeremiah 29:11, 1 Corinthians 10:13, Hebrews 13:5-6)

Acknowledging Our Sinfulness

When my daughter was in first grade, she talked a lot about "tallies" in our conversations about school. I was never really certain what she was referring to, but it was obvious they were very important to her.

One day the school had an open house. As I visited Jula's classroom I found that tallies were simply little pieces of colored paper. I was surprised at first, but as the teacher explained their use, I could see why they were so important to the children!

Each little colored slip of paper represented good or bad behaviors. Each child had his or her own "tally" jar. At the end of the day, rewards and punishments were given according to the "tallies" in each jar.

The words "black tally" would bring an instant hush to the classroom and a vast improvement in their conduct because this slip was saved for exceptionally bad behavior. The children all knew the punishment ahead for those who had black tallies in their jar. Three of them meant an immediate visit to the principal's office!

My daughter had been out of that class for several years, and I had forgotten about "tallies" until one autumn morning when I was in the school office. The door was thrown open and in marched Mrs. Robinson, the first grade teacher. She was towing two wiggly little boys.

As they were ushered in, I saw that one little boy was biting his lip to keep from crying, and the other boy was trying hard to look tough.

Mrs. Robinson marched them directly into the principal's office, placed them before the big desk and began to speak.

It seems school had only been in session for 15 minutes, yet these two perennial troublemakers had already collected two black tallies each. Knowing they would never get through the day without earning another one, they had come up with a plan to escape the consequences of a trip to the principal's office. They would destroy the evidence! Waiting until Mrs. Robinson's back was turned, they hurried up to the tally jars, took out the black slips of paper and proceeded to eat them. Unfortunately for them, the teacher turned back around too quickly and they were on their way to the principal's office much sooner than they had thought.

As I watched them squirm under the relentless questioning of the principal, I thought about how typical their actions were. We all feel the same way about the black tallies in our lives. We would rather not face the consequences either. Like those two little boys, we would rather "eat the evidence" by ignoring it and seeing if we can escape God.

Oh, how we hate exposure! We hug our cloaks of self-righteousness around ourselves like armor, pushing away any kind of probing that might reveal the roots of sin that lie underneath the surface, constantly keeping our lives in turmoil. Yet those black tallies of our sinfulness stand in the way of our relationship with God, rob us of peace and cause many of the difficult circumstances in which we find ourselves.

When we endeavor to acknowledge God in all our ways, it means we have to acknowledge God's right to bring discipline and chastisement. It means we have to submit to God's piercing light and acknowledge our sinfulness. It means we have to realize that we are guilty, not just of sinful acts, but of a basic sinful nature with which we must constantly deal. It all sounds so painful and threatening that we hesitate to submit to God in this part of our relationship. But actually, the problems our sinfulness causes are much more painful than the solution.

Our sin nature wants to keep us from walking in the path of repentance. Our carnality is fighting for its very existence. It will whisper, "You're not so bad," "Look at what they're guilty of," "God doesn't expect that!" "You're only human," and on and on. But the righteousness we like to hug to ourselves is nothing but self-delusion.

When we are in difficult situations, our carnal nature will be quick to "get rid of the tallies" by shifting the blame to other people, the economy, fate, and even God Himself, instead of allowing God's light to shine upon our own attitudes and our own propensity for sin.

When we are caught in a sin that threatens to destroy our lives, we are so busy pointing our fingers, saying, "They made me do it!" that we fail to face up to our responsibilities for our own actions.

When we are suffering terrifying financial reverses, we can be so busy explaining how it happened that we fail to face the sinful areas or the immaturities in our lives that may have brought us to that point.

When we are trying to recover from a broken relationship, we can be so busy trying to restore our damaged self-esteem that we don't want to face the areas where WE were wrong or the problems WE caused.

When we are struggling with the pain of being horribly wronged through no fault of our own, we can be so busy hugging our bitterness, self-pity and self-righteousness to ourselves that we fail to realize our reactions are rooted in the pride of "I shouldn't be treated this way!"

Our self-centeredness, our pride, our desire to please, our self-will, our selfishness, our demandingness, our apathy toward God — all will become more apparent when we choose to acknowledge God in all our ways, allowing His light to shine upon our sinful nature.

What does this have to do with trusting God? When sin lies between God and us, we are unable to rest in Him because the sin is usually getting us into problems over and over. At the same time, our spirit is convicting us and our carnal nature is expending enormous energy trying to ignore it. It is amazing how blind we can be in those situations. Often we can see no correlation between the problems we are in and our own sinfulness. It's the dilemma of our "understanding" again.

I recently watched a man bail out of a 20-year marriage. It was ironic that he chose to leave at the time he did. As a Christian, he had persevered for a long time in a difficult situation, but right about the time that God began to heal his emotionally-scarred wife, he became involved with someone else and left the marriage.

It was so senseless, until I realized that his wife's new growth and new capacity to love him were beginning to put pressure on him to deal with his own part of the problem. He had been able to shift the blame for years because her behavior had enabled him to be the victim in his own eyes, but now it was becoming impossible to keep up the wall and to keep from seeing his own wrong-doing. Rather than endure the scrutiny and look at the enormity of his own sin nature, he chose to throw away 20 years of serving God faithfully by stepping away from God and his marriage in order to pursue a different lifestyle.

Why do we hate the light of God so much? Why does it seem so terrible for that light to begin to shine upon the dark places and expose the hidden sin nature? We want so badly to keep our illusions about ourselves! Yet allowing God's piercing light to reveal the motives and intents of our hearts brings freedom and joy unlike anything we've ever known — joy as we let go of the pretending and the self-delusion, joy as we receive God's love and acceptance of us just as we are, and love and appreciation for Christ as we realize the enormity of our need for His sacrificial death on the cross.

* * *

When God decides to put His finger on areas of our lives that must come to the cross, He brings it to our attention through the teaching of His word or the prompting of His Spirit. If that fails, then He stops protecting us from the consequences of the sin.

When we choose to come to God over and over during problems with an open, submitted attitude instead of justifying ourselves, then we begin to exchange our understanding for His. Then as we see the sin that is at the root of our problem, we are able to repent and gain new insight and understanding. When we face difficult situations, we must learn to come quickly to God for examination instead of putting it off, blaming everyone else and ignoring God's prompting. We must be willing to see the sin He may be trying to reveal when He allows difficulties to come our way.

Of course not all of life's tough situations come because God is dealing with sin. That may not be the case at all. But when we are willing to acknowledge God in everything, His purpose will be revealed and we can come much more quickly into the good that God wants to accomplish in our lives.

When personal change is needed, our repentance and submission will bring us freedom from sin and the sin nature and will remove the hindrances to our relationship with God. We will be drawn closer to

Him in communion, fellowship and love; and in that place of closeness our heart again can rest in Him, trusting in His care and concern.

Exposing Sin

There are many problems we cannot be free of until we see and repent of the sin that is at the root of it. We have a tendency to want to clean up the outside, placing a veneer of righteousness over ourselves so that we look pretty good on the surface. However, problems, often relational, or an inability to gain victory over moral lapses, can be an indication of the need to allow God to examine what's really in our hearts.

The importance of living a life of repentance cannot be overstated. If you do not have the kind of relationship with God that includes a regular revealing of sin, or if God has never dealt with you about the root sins in your life, then I urge you to take time right now to tell Him you are willing to be shown your sin. Repentance is more than just an acknowledgment that we're sinful and sometimes sin. Sin must fill us with such revulsion that we are driven to our knees, filled with sorrow and a desire for change.

Each of us has root tendencies that need to be exposed by Christ's light so that we can repent and be changed. The hardest kind of sin to acknowledge is the kind that is wrapped up with deeply held hurts and bitterness. This kind of sin is often at the root of our relational problems: our unrealistic expectations of others, our relentless ambitions, our tendencies to self-protection, our all-consuming drive to satisfy unmet needs even when doing so runs counter to God's way, our preoccupation with ourselves and how we are treated.

What is God trying to show you today? What on-going problem have you been trying to figure out by looking outward and placing blame? Ask God to show you where your part of the problem is. Be open to examine any sin He wants to reveal to you.

Study

Read Jeremiah 2:30 and 35. What attitude did the people described in these Scriptures have? They were unrepentant
would not acknowledge their sin

What elements of repentance do the following Scriptures describe?

Hosea 14:1-2 forgiveness when there
is repentance

Lamentations 1:20 torment from lack
of repentance

Read 2 Corinthians 7:9-11. Have you ever experienced this kind of sorrow for sins? Godly sorrow leads to
repentance

Read Psalm 51:4. What knowledge/attitude must be present in true repentance? Our sin is against God

Read Psalm 139:23-24. Make this Scripture your prayer today.

Memorize

Create in me a pure heart, O God, and renew a steadfast spirit within me.
Psalm 51:10

Prayer of Response

Dear heavenly Father, I lay my heart open to You. Please examine me and reveal my sinfulness. Jesus, let me see myself in Your cleansing light. Probe, uncover and reveal what is really in my heart and let me see the sin for all that it is. I want to be free of the root sin of ____________________. Show me how deeply it permeates my life so I can repent and be set free. Jesus, thank You for dying on the cross so I can be forgiven and washed clean. Thank You for the resurrection power You give so I can have victory over sin. Amen.

Reflect

1. Look up Job 36:8-10. The first part of this Scripture describes the combination of sin and woundedness that is so often behind many of our problems. Yet what is necessary for change?
2. Which of the following is a root sin for you: willfulness, self-pity, concern for what other's think, pride or selfishness?

Acknowledging Our Pasts

"My parents gave me everything I wanted: nice clothes, a car when I was 16 and plenty of money, but all I ever wanted was for them to spend some time with me. They never attended any of my band concerts, and I think they only saw a handful of the Little League games I played in. They were always too busy."

"Both of my parents were alcoholics. I spent my childhood helping them home from bars, using the money from my paper route to buy food for my sisters and me and lying to teachers and friends about my home life."

"My father molested me from the time I was 8 until I was 15. How could God allow that?"

The stories of hurt and sorrow from painful childhoods are distressing. Of all those in the world who are innocently hurt, children are the most tragic. Our hearts ache at the stories of deprivation and abuse that some children have to bear. It really doesn't seem fair.

Yet, if we are to allow God to bring His good into the lives of those still-hurt people, we must again go to Him in acknowledgment. No, He did not cause it. His heart must be broken more by child abuse than by any other sin. Jesus was adamant about God's punishment for those who hurt little ones, but because He allows the world to go on in the course of sin-wrought destruction, children suffer.

However, God's remedy for that was included in Jesus' dying for us on the cross. Those who give their lives to God and accept Christ are able to receive healing, help and restoration of all that Satan robbed from them. Sometimes, though, the restoration is difficult to accomplish. The relationship that God wants to have with us is sometimes much harder to obtain for those who have been hurt as children or perhaps as adults.

All of us were born into a sinful world. We not only inherit a sin nature, but we each suffer from the effects of sin on our personalities. Some people were terribly mistreated as children. With others, relatively minor incidents caused deep scarring, while some came through childhood with little effect on their personalities. But our pasts can make a great deal of difference in our "understanding," and thus our ability to trust God.

For everyone, however, God desires restoration and wholeness. It is only as we are made whole in our personality that we can partake of the kind of relationship God desires to have with us, enabling us to trust Him, enabling us to understand His ways and walk in His path.

When people come to Jesus in salvation, the wounds from their pasts are not necessarily resolved. God cannot immediately make our whole lives wonderful or there would be no reason to seek Him, no reason to draw close and no opportunity for Him to develop a relationship with us. God wants to take those events that caused us so much damage and use them to bring beauty to our lives, but in this also we must begin to acknowledge Him.

We have to acknowledge His right in our lives in the fact that He did not stop the hurt from coming our way. We must acknowledge that He, in His infinite wisdom and foreknowledge, saw the result and the good that He could bring from those very scars that seemed to mar our lives.

With some, acknowledging God becomes the first step in trusting God because their pasts make it difficult for them to believe that God really loves them. It makes it difficult to really trust in a God who allowed the hurts they had to suffer. Even though they are able to come to Him in salvation, their subsequent relationships with Him may be thwarted again and again by their own pasts, and their own understanding.

They believe in God. They believe He is good, but their pasts keep the knowledge they have of God from filtering down into their emotions. The knowledge cannot get past "the understanding." God has to deal with each one individually in order to bring wholeness, drawing people to a closer relationship where they can trust Him enough to open themselves and their pasts to Him for His healing touch.

Often, God cannot deal effectively with sin or teach His principles of trust until He has brought some degree of restoration to the personality. This may be the reason that some people seem to "get away" with questionable behavior patterns or worldly lifestyles for so long. God is, many times, patiently working to bring healing before He can deal with the sin. But He knows how to bring pressure to bear in just the right way and at just the right time to cause each of us to see our needs for help.

We, in turn, must open ourselves up to Him, to begin to acknowledge God by submitting to Him in all things. As we begin to submit to God, He can use the turmoil and problems to reveal our need for healing. By dealing with Him in all things that are part of our lives, big or small, we acknowledge Him and He can reveal areas of our life that are in need of healing, correction and restoration.

Often, our pasts continue to disrupt our present. Sometimes we see the pattern, but just as often we do not. Sometimes our pasts cause us to carry misconceptions and distortions about God. We often project upon Him characteristics and actions that are mistaken and distorted.

It takes God time to bring truth and healing into our lives, but He can accomplish wonderful things.

Stormie Omartian's autobiography, *Stormie,* is an excellent example of personal healing. The book shares her odyssey from a traumatic childhood through the painful problems it caused and her desperate need for help, to her salvation and subsequent healing. One of the most important aspects of the book, however, is that it reveals the methodical and patient way God brought about restoration.

First, Stormie purposed in her heart to go to God for help and that was the key to her healing. Because of that recurring commitment to acknowledge God in all her ways by seeking Him in each new situation, God was able to bring His ultimate good into her life. Time after time, as her past created problems for her present, she would take the problems and her past to God for His insight and healing. In it all, she was acknowledging God by submitting to Him for His help and insight. The healing and release didn't always come about quickly. He used other people, His Word, her own faith and many different circumstances to accomplish His plan of restoration.

Although many of us did not suffer debilitating abuse as children, we do have negative response patterns that began in our childhoods, sometimes because of the unwitting errors by our parents or another significant person in our lives.

I had a relatively good childhood, but a few years ago I finally reached a point, during a situation that seemed a repetition of other incidents, that I finally cried out to God, "Why does this always happen? Why do I always react this way?" As I sought God, He immediately brought to mind a minor, unintentional pattern of treatment by my parents that had started the whole cycle. As it all came into amazing clarity, I began to cry bitter tears of hurt and grief for the pain they had ignorantly inflicted. I grieved over it for about three days, my mind going back to it easily as I went through my daily routine. Each time I asked for God's healing and each day the pain lessened until I was able to think about it without grief. Then, as the sorrow passed, it all settled back into place as part of my background, my "acknowledged and understood" background. I have never grieved over it again. The problems it caused are gone.

I had accepted that particular treatment by my parents as normal and deserved, and although it had bothered me as a child, I didn't think much about it. It was only with the help of the Holy Spirit that I was able to see the distorted response pattern it had created.

God wants to give us abundant life so that our relationships with Him and other people are unhindered by scars and distortions from our pasts. But He is unable to help us in this area until we begin to acknowledge Him in situations that we face; until we are willing to seek His face, acknowledging the problem and our need. For every person who recognizes the trauma of their childhood there are countless others who have put it away, who see no correlation between the problems they may be having in their lives, and their past experiences or relationships.

My husband and I have been friends with John and Sally for a number of years. It is interesting to listen to the differences in the ways they refer to John's childhood.

John always speaks of his youth in glowing terms, describing it as a wonderful, all-American childhood.

Sally, however, is amazed by his overall memory of it because she knows many of the details. As she relates it, his parents were uncaring and in many ways abusive.

In order to deal with painful reality, many children cope by accepting the lifestyle and manner in which they were treated as either normal or deserved. They reach adulthood thinking that a certain way of life is the norm, or they conclude that "they" were to blame. Often they take on the same way of life: they continue to use the same defense mechanisms they developed in childhood; they continue to see situations, other people and themselves with the same warped perspectives; and they continue to apply the same distorted logic they developed as children to their adult relationships and situations. The pattern goes on because often they don't think they have a problem – everyone else does.

For many people, it is easier to cope with distorted perceptions learned as a child than it is to deal with the past. We'd rather go on in the patterns than acknowledge we have a problem. So we become locked in behaviors, problems and distorted thinking. Again and again, our pasts, or the misguided thinking which began in our pasts, creates problems for our present.

I am definitely not advocating excessive introspection and preoccupation with ourselves, our behaviors and our pasts. But willing and submissive hearts will enable us to find insight and healing when it is needed.

There seem to be two basic philosophies regarding inner healing: One is that we must deal profusely with the events of our past. The other is that we need to simply put it behind us and go on with Christ. Somewhere between those two extremes lies God's plan for us. We must be willing for God to show us if we have a need in this area. We must seek His direction and submit to the counsel of the Holy Spirit. God knows our temperament, our needs and the purpose He has planned for our lives, and He knows the path of healing that is best for us. Our tendency will be, like the two extremes, to either wallow in it or to completely ignore it. We need God's divine enablement to bring His perception, His light, His healing and His plan to our lives.

Often we are not aware that our pasts are affecting our present lives and our relationships with God. Perhaps we have forgotten or pushed away incidents that still continue to lie unhealed beneath the surface of our consciousness, keeping our understanding and our reactions clouded by our pasts. We must be willing to acknowledge God in this area also, to seek His face and allow Him to reveal anything that might be affecting us. If we continually struggle with relationships or are unable to find victory over sin, if we are trapped by compulsive behavior or are constantly battling feelings of fear, worthlessness or guilt, then we should begin to seek God's understanding and insight. We must acknowledge Him by giving ourselves to Him for His help and healing.

Each of us must realize that God didn't cause the painful things in our past. A sinful world did that. But if He allowed it, He will bring good as we learn to acknowledge Him in it. God may have already brought good by using your past to bring you to Him. Often the very scars that mar our lives, making us vulnerable and needy, are the cause of our coming to Christ. Or it may be the reason we are so dependent upon Him: the evil that came our way through no fault of our own forces our character into a dependency on God that we would never have had in other circumstances.

But God has a greater good to give. He desires to free us from the distorted response patterns in our life. He wants to free us from seeing situations through the warped and darkened windows of our past. He wants to enable us to see as He sees, to understand with His understanding and be whole.

Whatever the good that God will bring, our acknowledgment of Him must take place so that He is free to give to us all the good only He could salvage out of pain. We must be willing to acknowledge that God allowed it into our lives, and as we submit to Him, He will redeem our pasts and bring good from them. He will heal us from the pain of our pasts and free us from the power they have over us to continue to disrupt and hurt our lives.

Then we will be free to see God as He really is, to come into the fullness of relationship with Him that will be our highest joy, and to live in peace and rest as we trust in Him.

Painful Pasts

Perhaps you have resisted opening up your past to God's light, thinking it is unnecessary. Yet, in all honesty, you admit to on-going relationship problems or an inability to overcome certain behavior patterns or sins.

Perhaps thinking about your past is too painful to try. Whether you are thinking, "It won't do any good," or "It's just not worth the pain," or some other kind of self-protective thinking, I urge you now to submit yourself to God in this area. There may be momentary pain involved as old wounds are reopened, but you need God's insight to help you see how your past is affecting your present. You need to see why you are locked into distorted thought patterns, unrealistic expectations, uncontrollable behaviors, moral problems or unrelenting relationship problems.

Study

Read Colossians 1:13. What have we been delivered from?

...he has rescued us from the power of darkness

Read 2 Corinthians 3:17. What do we have because of the Spirit of the Lord in us? we are set free

Even though we may not have clear understanding about how our past affects our present, what does Hebrews 4:13 say about God's knowledge? everything lies naked and exposed before the eyes of God.

What does Hebrews 12:15 say about things that are hidden?

Mark 4:22 nothing is hidden, except to be revealed; nor has anything been secret but it should come to light!

Write out the promises we can claim based on the Scriptures below as we receive healing from the wounds of our past.

Psalm 147:3 He heals the broken hearted and binds up their wounds

Ephesians 2:14 He is our peace

Isaiah 26:3 perfect peace if we trust in Him.

Joel 2:32 Whoever calls on the name of the Lord will be delivered

Luke 10:19 nothing shall injure you

Read Psalm 43:1-5. What does verse 3 say that we need if we are to walk in healing and wholeness? light and truth

Memorize

And the peace of God, which transcends all understanding, will guard your hearts and your minds in Christ Jesus.

Phillipians 4:7

Prayer of Response

Dear Father, I believe You love me and only want good for me, so I submit to You in this area. Although the thought of dealing with my past seems more than I can do, I am willing to be made willing. I ask for Your help. I know I can leave this in Your hands and trust You to bring good into my life. Amen.

Reflect

1. If there is something from your past that you know is still affecting your present, consider sharing it with someone.
2. If you have already received healing for past hurts, share your experience of receiving help and healing.
3. Pray for a friend who is hurting from and/or dealing with his or her past.

Acknowledging God Daily

Our car is only a few years old and it's a nice car. I like it. The left back door has a slight rattle in it sometimes, but it doesn't bother me. Actually, I don't usually hear it.

My daughter does, though, and it really irritates her. She fidgets and turns and makes loud sighing noises until she finally can't control herself.

"That door is driving me crazy!"

I patiently answer, "Really? I hadn't noticed it today. Is it rattling again?"

"You can't hear that?" she queries suspiciously.

"No…well, yes, now I do."

"Then when are you going to get it fixed?" she demands.

"It's hard to find rattles, Jula," I say for the hundredth time.

"Well, can't they replace the door?" She continues to pursue the argument, but by now my patience is wearing thin.

"Oh, sure, next time I get a tune-up, I'll tell them to replace the back door!"

Determined to have the last word, she answers, "It IS irritating, Mom."

"Yes, I know. Just don't let it bother you."

I know she hates to hear that. We all do. There's a lot in our lives that annoys us: cars that won't start, snarled traffic, fussy kids, long lines at cash registers, bad hair cuts and bad drivers. Yet we are all faced with the command to "acknowledge God in all our ways." Even our daily annoyances? That's tough!

Yet, it is our daily responses to people and life's situations that is the essence of who we are and where we are in our relationship with God. It is here that the groundwork is laid for minor things to escalate into major problems. It is here that our real submission to God is revealed, and it is here that we are set up for the situations and problems that lie in our future.

Our relationship with our Father God never stops. It is day by day, and moment by moment. It isn't just in the bad days when we must cling to Him, but it's also in the good days when we're praising Him, and in the mundane — drop the kids at school, pick up a loaf of bread on the way home from work — days of our lives.

When we refuse to acknowledge God in our daily lives, we are saying yes to our natural responses, our natural reactions and our natural way of doing things. Many of these responses may be just fine, but some will be the source of problems ahead. Some are actually just the tip of the iceberg. Underneath the surface lie the root problems that so disrupt our lives. God knows the areas that will be our downfall. As we submit to Him daily, He is able to deal with us daily and begin to help us with our weaknesses.

Paul called this way of life "walking in the spirit." Although it isn't possible to pray over every thought or decision, it is possible to be submitted to God in our hearts and be willing to trust Him. We can consciously make the decision to submit our lives to Him — all of our lives — every day. As we submit our daily lives to God, He will enable us to walk in His spirit so that our reactions reflect the kind of response God would give.

As we submit daily, we begin to learn lessons about ourselves — our sinfulness, our weaknesses and the areas where we need to grow up spiritually — and these lessons will keep us from having to learn the hard way. God will use the easiest path He can to teach us His principles and draw us into a relationship with Him. Those who have learned to acknowledge Him in all ways will come much easier to a life of trust and rest in God.

Samuel Hayakawa, the former U.S. Senator from California, tells of living in Chicago earlier in his life and daily riding the street cars. He had to ride on a streetcar line that traveled down an avenue that was often blocked by badly parked cars and huge trucks trying to maneuver. Some of the motormen would get red with rage at the delays, clanging their bells and shouting at the drivers. At the end of the day, they were probably nervous wrecks, jittery and angry. Other motormen, however, would sit and wait quietly while delayed. Never getting impatient, they calmly whistled a tune, cleaned their fingernails or wrote their reports.

The two sets of motormen were confronted with the same objective situation. However, one set lived a hellish life of anger and nervous tension; the other had a relaxing job, with plenty of time for rest.

Interesting contrast, isn't it? Same situation, but vastly different responses. What a difference it can make in the quality of a life!

God wants us to carry out our lives in peace, joy and contentment, but many times we don't do that. We're too busy clanging the bells, shaking our fists, and complaining about the rattles. Our natural responses to life keep us in turmoil and anger, impatience and frustration. Instead of a peace-filled life based on a relationship of trust in God, we spend our days fretting and stewing, reacting to the situations of our day with frustration, impatience, anger and self-pity.

If we see the necessity of acknowledging God's hand in the unchangeable events that have disrupted our lives, bringing turmoil and pain, we still may fail to see that acknowledging God is not just for those life-changing circumstances, but also for the daily events of our lives. The snarled traffic, the burned dinner, the forgotten key — the daily upheavals and disappointments — these, too, need to be brought to God as we acknowledge Him.

Much of the good that comes from learning to trust God and learning His principles is for the very purpose of enabling us to live day by day in a trusting, peace-filled life. Yet, if we never take those principles of trust, acceptance or acknowledgment of His sovereignty and begin to apply them to our every day lives, then we are missing the point. God has in mind a day-by-day relationship. It is daily that we are to "know" Him.

When we begin to "know" Him day by day, by acknowledging Him, then we will begin to experience the kind of life He desires for us. We will learn to respond to life's daily situations with the fruit of the Spirit instead of the reactions of the flesh. Like the motormen facing the same situations but reacting differently, we too should begin to see change in our daily lives.

With each person the need is different, but for all of us the answer lies in our acknowledgment of God in our daily lives and our acknowledgment of our need for Him to help us in every situation, no matter how big or small it may be. Whether the need is for self-discipline or patience, whether we are in need of wisdom or loving kindness, all are ours as we begin to seek God in our daily lives and receive His good in us.

When we learn to acknowledge God, submitting to His lordship every day, we are doing the most positive and effective things we can do to bring peace and joy into our lives. As we submit and acknowledge Him, we free Him to work in and through us daily. He will give us the grace we need in difficult days, the insight we need in confusing days and the help we need every day to be better husbands, wives, parents, employees and friends.

Day by Day

We can all see God in exceptional things, but it requires the growth of spiritual discipline to see God in every detail. Never believe that the so-called random events of life are anything less than God's appointed order. Be ready to discover His divine design anywhere and everywhere.

—Oswald Chambers, *My Utmost for His Highest*

Study

What does Psalm 118:24 say about our "day"? ____________________

____

____

Read Colossians 3:17. What are we to do in the name of Jesus?

____

____

____

Read Proverbs 16:3. What are we to commit to the Lord?

____

____

Read Matthew 13:22. What did Jesus say would choke the Word of God in us? ____

____

____

Memorize

The steps of a good man are ordered by the Lord, and He delights in his way.
Psalm 37:23

Prayer of Response

Dear heavenly Father, thank You for being with me day by day and moment by moment. Help me to begin to learn to turn my daily life over to You so that You can begin to help me be more Christlike in my responses to life's upsets. And, Lord, I so often fail to appreciate all You do for me and forget how very faithful You are to me in the small things of my life. Thank You for Your lovingkindness to me in the details of my life. Amen.

Reflect

This week, make an effort to acknowledge God in the small areas of your life. Thank Him for small blessings. Ask for His help in small crises. Ask for whichever fruit of the Spirit you need right then. Slow down your thinking as much as possible and take time to see these moments of your life as ordered by God and as opportunities to be with Him.

Acknowledging God's Care

On and on the days of our lives pass by, with jobs and responsibilities, needs and concerns, hopes and dreams, and daily routines. There is a great deal of the mundane in my life and yours. Should we acknowledge God in all of it? Couldn't that get overwhelming?

"Does God want me to pray over the socks I pick out each morning? Should I ask whether or not I should eat corn flakes for breakfast, and which way I should drive to work, or what time I should eat lunch? Is that what it means to acknowledge God in all my ways!?!"

"But I can't be in prayer all day long!"

Our minds will make thousands of decisions daily from "I think I'll water the plants," to "I'm going to quit my job and start my own company." Where on the scale from trivial to life-changing does God become interested, and how do we figure it out? Is He interested in any of it — or all of it? Is that what "all my ways" (Proverbs 3:6) means?

What parts do my own intelligence and my personal choice play in my life? Where does God's will end and my ability to think begin?

If acknowledging God in all my ways means submission to Him in the choices and actions of my life, just how far does this go?

When God created people, He placed His own spirit within us to energize, direct and motivate. We were free to choose whether to submit to that spirit or to our own powerful abilities. When Adam's sin broke the union between God and people, human minds, emotions and wills became so overdeveloped that even after accepting Christ and joining our spirit back to God, our souls want to continue to work independently. Because we have lived "in control" for so long, we still want to use our own mind, will and emotions to pattern our lives. We are always free to do so, however God knows that a correct relationship with Him is the only chance for happiness.

God doesn't want puppets, but He does want to show us what life within "His" design can be. We will still use the mind God gave us. Our abilities to reason and plan do not become redundant. God takes a great deal of pleasure in our abilities. He wants His spirit within us, however, to be the energizing force behind those abilities, enabling us to be all that God created us to be.

When we acknowledge God in all our ways, what exactly does that mean? It really isn't possible to pray over every thought or decision. Yet it is possible to live in an attitude of submission. It isn't a matter of not using my brain to think and decide. It's a matter of first acknowledging His right over my life, over it all!

If I do acknowledge God in all my ways, then I acknowledge God's right over my life in all areas; from what I eat this morning to the important decision I will make this afternoon. Acknowledging God is submitting to God in my will and in my attitude. Although it isn't possible to pray over every thought or decision, it is possible to be submitted to God in our hearts, willing to trust Him. We can consciously make the decision to submit our lives to Him — all of our lives, every day.

For many, it is easier to just say that God isn't concerned with the "ways of my life," because that lets us off the hook. I do not have to endeavor to submit to His Lordship in the areas in which I say He is not concerned. It's tempting to say that the choice of a spouse, career, house, vacation and so on are our responsibilities, and God is responsible only for the spiritual part of our lives so we do not need to acknowledge God in all our ways.

We can choose to run our own lives because…

"that's why God gave me a mind," or

"God isn't interested in that," or

"God is only concerned with the eternal aspects of my life."

Our reasons for not acknowledging God in all our ways can become quite articulate and logical. However, it boils down to the fact that we do not want to submit our lives totally to His control. We want to take a vacation when we want to, buy the things we choose and do the things we want to do.

Many areas and decisions of our lives God obviously leaves up to us. There is probably no clear will of God on whether you eat corn flakes or muffins for breakfast. However, if God is dealing with you about an eating problem in your life, He may be interested in that decision, and His spirit may speak to you about it. We decide whether we will submit our will and acknowledge Him in that area.

Our root problem as humans has always been our desire to trust in ourselves instead of God. The part of us that holds back from God, that clings to the desire for our own way, is convinced that we know what is best. The truth is that we don't. God designed and created us and knows what is best for each of our lives (all the way down to the color of socks we wear). When we have decided to "walk in the Spirit," we can leave it to God to reveal to us those areas with which He is concerned.

Our relationship with our Father God never stops. It is day by day, and moment by moment. It isn't just in the bad days when we must cling to Him, but it's also in the good days when we're praising Him, and in the mundane days of our lives.

This relationship isn't just for spiritual moments. It's for every moment! God's desire when He created us was for fellowship — a continual relationship — and His actions throughout history have always revealed His interest and involvement in all of our ways.

In the Old Testament we see evidence of God's provision and interest in the daily affairs of His children: He sent ravens to feed Elijah, He raised an axhead out of the water that needed to be returned to a neighbor, He helped a shepherd boy kill a lion to protect the sheep and He sent manna to the hungry Israelites.

In the New Testament, Jesus reminded us that God is our Father. If He cared about the flowers of the field and the birds of the air, Jesus said, wouldn't He also care about every aspect of our lives, down to the hairs on our head?

If we are to "know" God in all our ways, we must first be convinced that God is concerned with "all our ways." We must begin to know that God, who walked with Enoch and talked with Moses, is interested in all that concerns us.

* * *

My husband, Chuck, had only been out of college for a few years, our second child had been born a few months before, and we were still struggling to pay the doctor and hospital bills, when the invitation to my 10-year high school class reunion arrived.

We traveled back for the reunion that summer, staying with my parents for the weekend. We had only been there a few hours when my mother asked to see the dress I had brought to wear to the formal Saturday night dinner.

As I showed her the dress, she tried to hide her chagrin, but I knew how she felt. Clothes and appearance had been important to me while growing up, but attending college during the hippie era had done a lot to change that. Now, even if I wanted to be concerned about my wardrobe, marriage, two pregnancies and babies to care for meant I did not have the time or money to spend on clothes.

However, being faced with seeing all my old friends was enough to make me long for something new. When my best friend brought over the gorgeous dress she had bought for the occasion, my longing quickly grew more intense. I knew, though, that our finances precluded me from being able to do anything about it.

Two old friends wanted to go shopping the day of the reunion like we used to, so with Mom taking care of the kids, we started out for a day of fun and nostalgia. My parents were having financial problems at the time, too, but as I walked out the door, my mom pressed $10 into my hand.

"I know it isn't much, but maybe you'll find something you like today," she said.

"Thanks, Mom," I called as I ran out the door to join the girls. I put the money in my wallet and forgot about it. Ten dollars wasn't really going to help, but my delight in the outing with old friends overshadowed much of the concern about clothes for that night.

And we did have fun! We visited the stores where we had shopped as teenagers when we had babysitting money to spend. We tried on clothes, looked at makeup, laughed and talked. We ate lunch at the same greasy cafe that served great hamburgers, forgetting about the "health food" we were all now eating.

After lunch, my friend Donna, who still lived in that town, said, "Hey, there's a new outlet for designer clothes down on Pine Street. Let's go there."

We piled into the car and headed over to look at the aisles of clothes, trying on those that caught our eye and laughing as we tried to see who could find the most outrageous outfits.

We stopped to glance through the clearance rack before leaving, and there, way in the back, out of place amidst the odd assortment of colors and styles that had failed to sell through countless markdowns, was a long, beautiful dress. I looked it over with disbelief before I finally took it to the dressing room to try on.

It fit perfectly, flowing to the floor. The color showed off my tan, the style hid the post pregnancy bulges, and it cost…$10!

When I got home, I ran in to show Mom the dress. She started to cry as she told me that she had gone into her bedroom after I left and knelt down to ask God for a favor: "Please, Father, help her to find a pretty dress. It is important to her. I know she wants to look nice." Our heavenly Father, who really does care about such things, had already taken care of it, keeping that dress through markdown after markdown until the moment I walked into the store.

I still have the dress. It's out of style now, but I still love to look at it. It always reminds me of God's care and concern for me in the little things of my life.

Aware of Care

We sometimes feel, "Is He really concerned with my daily affairs — the need to get a job assignment done, my desire for a raise, my hope for a new car, the struggle to land new accounts at work, my inability to find the error in the books? Is He concerned?"

Are YOU concerned?

If so, then yes, God is concerned. Would a God who desired a relationship with you so much that He sent His son to die for you, not also care about every part of your existence, desiring to be a part of your life and a source of help to you in every area?

The Holy Spirit He imparts to each of us is His very Spirit, given to comfort, guide and help. He is there for us. Whether or not we make use of His help is our decision. But He is present within us. He is a part of the whole of our lives, not just the spiritual.

Nothing in our lives is outside of God's sphere of concern or control. His interest is not limited to just those things that further our Christian character or bring glory to Him. He cares about it all. Lived in submission to Him, our lives bring Him glory whether we're mowing the lawn or witnessing to a friend.

He has told us not to worry over the daily matters of our lives, clothing and food, because He will take care of us. We are to set our minds upon Him. That means knowing Him in all of it. Day after day we can be aware of His presence and help in every aspect of our lives. He wants us to recognize His care and trust in Him as we acknowledge Him in all our ways.

Study

Read Zechariah 4:10. Write out a paraphrase of this verse.

____

____

____

Read Matthew 6:26. What small thing does God feed?

____

Read Matthew 6:28. What small thing does God clothe?

____

Read Matthew 10:30. What small thing does God number?

____

Read 2 Kings 6:1-7. What small item did God recover?

____

Read Psalm 68:19. What does God do daily?

____

Memorize

How priceless is your unfailing love! Both high and low among men find refuge in the shadow of your wings.
Psalm 36:7

Prayer of Response

Dear heavenly Father, I do want to acknowledge You in all my ways by trusting You with all my life. Forgive me for holding back areas, and Lord, forgive the lack of trust in You that causes me to hold them back. Go down deep and remove the root of unbelief, the inability to believe You are good all the time and will always be good to me. I want to trust You with all of my life. Amen.

Reflect

1. Think about a time when God helped you with something small.
2. Is there an area of your life you have kept off limits to God in the past, saying to yourself "He isn't interested"?
3. Is the Spirit of God speaking to you now about anything you have refused to acknowledge Him in?
4. Is it time to submit to God "all" of your life, every decision, every choice? Are you ready to place all under His authority?

Part Four

And He Shall Direct Your Paths

Trusting Our Paths to God

My friend Jim loves to tell the story about the time he took his son David and his nephew Keith on the boat ride at Disneyland. The boys were about 5 years old at the time and had been begging to ride on the boats. The boat ride at Disneyland is similar to the car rides that are in many amusement parks. The children can steer the boats themselves and enjoying "driving" like mom and dad. A rail underneath keeps the boat on a secure path.

As Jim got into the boat with Keith and David, the kids decided that they would take turns "driving." Keith was first, so he sat in front, gripped the big steering wheel, pushed down on the gas pedal and carefully began to steer the boat out into the open water.

As Keith settled into his job, Jim noticed the intense concentration on his face. He decided to make the ride as real as possible for the boys.

Leaning over the seat, he began to call out directions. "You need to turn toward the bank, Keith. Look out for that boulder over there."

"Now you need to make this turn sharply!"

Getting into the adventure of it, Jim's voice became more intense. "Look out, Keith! Don't hit that bank!"

"You'll have to turn hard here. Quickly, or we're going to hit the bank!"

Keith hurriedly turned the wheel as hard as he could, looking over at Jim anxiously.

"Wow, that was close!" Jim said, relief showing in his voice. "Now, watch out for those other boats." Pointing out obstacles and calling out directions, he continued to try to make the ride real.

Little Keith clutched the wheel with intensity, worry written all over his face. David, sitting on the other side, was very quiet while Jim kept up a steady stream of directions, "Look out, there's a sharp curve! OH, NO, WE'RE GOING TO HIT! Wow, we just made it!"

When they were about halfway, Jim turned to David and said, "Okay, it's your turn."

David didn't look at his Dad. Shrugging his shoulders, he quietly said, "Uhhh…I don't think I want to drive."

Jim was surprised. David had been so excited about driving the boat earlier! Jim looked over at Keith with his hands clutching the wheel and his eyes glued to the front, then back at David anxiously watching. Suddenly he realized what had happened. He had played his part so effectively that he had taken all the joy out of the ride for the boys. They thought it was for real!

Keith was nervously trying to do his best while David sat beside him, sweating it out as he watched, dreading his own turn at "responsibility."

Jim casually said, "You know, you can't even see the rail underneath the water, can you?" and, nonchalantly, he began to explain how the ride worked.

The boys listened intently as Keith continued to steer. In a few minutes, David spoke up, "I think I'll drive now."

All the trauma had been taken out of the ride when the boys realized they were not responsible for keeping their boat on course. It couldn't and wouldn't crash into the obstacles around them. They could settle in and enjoy the ride.

Some of us view our Christian lives the same way David and

Keith viewed the boat ride. We bring to our Christian walk the same drive, the same intensity, the same push to do it right that we've put into our lives for so many years. We strive to be "perfect" Christians and do everything right. When we inevitably find that we can't, we struggle with feelings of defeat and worthlessness.

The pressure of trying to get through our Christian lives is too much for us. We know ourselves. We know we're going to blow it. We worry because we know that we are our biggest problem, and we cry with Paul, "I find this law at work: When I want to do good, evil is right there with me." (Romans 7:21) Our only consistency is our inconsistency. We're stirred to change today, but tomorrow we don't feel like it. We determine to do better next time, only to make the same mistake again. We end up listening to Satan whisper, "What's the use? You can't do it. You're going to crash into the bank."

We have yet to learn that not only can we trust God with the circumstances of our lives, we can trust God with ourselves. He really does have it all under control. He will not allow us to get too far off course. God in us is greater than our inconsistency, our hot and cold desire to walk in His path. All along God is right there with His hand underneath us, guiding us. He knows He will get us through life's course. If our "boat" bumps a rock, it won't wreck it. If we miss a turn, God has another turn up ahead. He knows the way to get us there. If we mess up, He'll take another route, but He will accomplish what He desires.

God wants you to understand that He can take care of you, that He is bigger than your inability to serve Him consistently. He also wants you to understand that the work Christ did on the cross was a complete work. It was not just for your salvation, but for your sanctification (the working out of your salvation).

Every grace you need in your Christian walk, whether it is the fruit of the Spirit, victory over sin or the ability to trust during difficult times is yours because of Jesus Christ and His work on the cross, His resurrection and His life in you.

How can I impart to you the incredible wonder and the awesome reality that Jesus, who was and is God incarnate, lives in you?

Jesus — the same Jesus who healed the sick, fed the multitude and lived a perfect life in absolute, trusting obedience to our Father lives in us. He is God and "...through His Spirit who dwells in you" (Romans 8:11) we have divinity in us to empower us, to set us free from sin and to enable us to live a life of joy and peace as we walk in companionship and intimacy with the Father.

We can relax and enjoy the ride! Our part is simply to be in the "boat" of our relationship with God. What a blessed relief to feel the pressure and the responsibility taken off our shoulders and put back on God, where it belongs.

We can trust God with our lives.

A New Creature

Are you struggling with failure in your Christian walk? Is your inability to do and be all you feel God expects of you weighing you down?

Understanding that He "has given us everything we need for life and godliness" (2 Peter 1:3) is absolutely vital to you. If you have not yet grasped this truth, it is important that you spend time in God's Word reviewing the Scriptures until this truth permeates your being.

Prayerfully read Romans 6. This portion of Scripture changed my life at a time when I was struggling to overcome the carnality that seemed to dominate me. I was finally able to see that Christ had already done the work necessary for me to live a consistent Christian life, I just needed to know it. I was finally able to grasp that when He died on the cross, my sin had died with Him. It had no power over me anymore. I just hadn't realized it yet.

I also hadn't grasped that when Christ was raised from the dead, I was raised with Him — a new creature with power over sin! God knows that not only can we not save ourselves (we need a Savior), we also cannot sanctify ourselves. Christ must do it through us, and He will!

Study

Look up the following Scriptures and underline them in your Bible:

1 Thessalonians 5:23-24

1 Peter 1:5

Philippians 2:13

Read Romans 14:4. What does the last part of this verse say? Do you believe it for yourself? ______________________________

____

Read Ephesians 2:8-10. What does verse 10 say we are?

____

Read 2 Corinthians 1:21. In whom and by whom are we established?

____

Look up Philippians 1:6. In your Bible, substitute your name for "you" as you read. Meditate on that Scripture this week. In Ephesians 3:20, substitute "me" for "us" as you read.

Look up Philippians 4:19. The word "need" is often used to denote financial need. In light of the emphasis in this chapter, what other need could it mean? ______________________________

Read Romans 6 several times during the week. Ask God to make real to you the truths in this chapter.

Memorize

Being confident of this very thing, that He who has begun a good work in you will complete it until the day of Jesus Christ.
Philippians 1:6 (NKJV)

Prayer of Response

Dear Jesus, I need to know that the work You did on the cross was for my total salvation, not just to save me from sin and death but to save me from myself! Jesus, You have set me free from the power of sin and my old sin nature. Help me to grasp that fact — to count it so as Romans 6:11 says — while You work it out in my life. Thank You for Your gift of love and sacrifice to me. Amen.

Reflect

Do you need to grasp the truths of Romans 6? Is there something from which you need to be set free? Pray with a friend that you may both learn to "know" (believe it is already accomplished) the work of salvation and deliverance Christ has accomplished in and for you.

Decisions, Decisions, Decisions

There it was: a shiny red convertible with a great big "For Sale by Owner" sign on it, parked just where Chuck would see it on the very day we were to sign the lease on a practical blue sedan, almost identical to the one I had been driving for five years.

He called me excitedly. "You've got to see the car I just saw on the side of the road with a for sale sign on it. It's a red Mustang convertible, two years old, with only 10,000 miles."

Immediately, I asked, "What color of top does it have?"

"I'm not sure. The top was down and I didn't notice," he answered. "Why don't I pick you up and we'll go look at it?"

An hour later, we were on our way to see the car, trying not to be too excited. "I don't know, Chuck, do you think we should do this? It's a totally different kind of car."

"Deb, it's up to you. It will be your car. I only told you about it, because I know you've always wanted a red convertible."

"A red convertible with a white top," I corrected. (Most red convertibles have black tops.)

We discussed on the way to see the car that the fact that he saw it the same day we were to close the deal on the other car might be a factor. Maybe this was the car we were supposed to have.

As we rounded the corner and saw the car, I smiled. It was shiny, it was red, it was a convertible, and it had…a white top! This had to be the car for us. It was actually less expensive than the one we were going to buy, and the kids (Matt was 17 and Jula was 15) would be thrilled.

After a few minutes of chit-chat, the owner handed me the keys and suggested I take it for a drive. When I squealed the tires taking off, Chuck laughed and said I would have to get used to the tight clutch and a bigger engine. He also warned me, "This car definitely has a lot of horsepower. It has a 5.0 liter engine."

No problem. That didn't really mean anything to me. I just knew this would be a fun car and I kept thinking about how surprised our kids would be.

In my excitement, I barely listened as Chuck and the owner discussed the price. I nodded my head yes when Chuck looked over at me and before I knew it we had a new car. Not just a new car but a red convertible with a white top! Of course it also had a large powerful engine and a light body, but at that moment that didn't mean anything to me..

However, 10 months and two accidents later it meant everything. We sold the car the day it came out of the body shop for the second time, thankful beyond words that neither of our children had been hurt. This car had been a lethal combination: a powerful engine, a convertible and two inexperienced, teenage drivers. The second accident happened the very first day Jula drove it to school after she got her license.

What had we been thinking?

But 10 months before all I could see was a shiny red convertible with a white top.

* * *

In the last chapter we looked at our security in the fact that God will direct our paths as we submit to Him. However, this does not mean we will not have to make choices or we'll never think about another decision. Acknowledging God in everything and trusting in His divine care is not passive acquiescence or blind faith. We are never to accept all that life throws at us with an attitude of resignation, thinking, *Oh well, this must be God's will for me.*

There will be choices to make, crossroads to face and alternate paths to consider throughout our lives. There will be consequences from the choices we make!

Satan watches the pathways we are on and carefully watches our reactions. He can easily tell when and where we're vulnerable to shiny red convertibles. He never hesitates to use every insight into our character that he has in order to bring just the right kind of circumstance to distract us from God's path for us.

There are certain times when we are more susceptible to distraction. They are usually times of great discouragement or times of apparent success. When we are in the throes of discouraging circumstances and the seductive pull of unfulfilled dreams or human needs, often a new path will suddenly appear leading off in another direction. Just when we have begun to lean more on God, spend more time in prayer and the Word and begun to allow God to deal in our lives — that is the time a bright, new, seemingly innocuous pathway appears on the horizon.

Therefore, it is imperative that the things that come across our paths be examined with prayerful attention. We can never just lazily assume everything that comes our way is from God because it looks good to us or because it seems to come at opportune times. There will always be Delilahs, Bathshebas, shiny red convertibles and a snake sitting by a fruit tree in the middle of a garden.

Yet the choices we face and the decisions we sometimes agonize over are not sent to trip us up, but to bring us to God, allowing Him to provide the help we need to stay on His path. Choices should not be a snare to our feet, but stepping stones to new knowledge of God. God knows what is best for us and He wants us to know too. He has faithfully provided help for us to enable us to walk on His path for us.

I took a hike with some friends the other day along a new trail on a mountain in our area. There were four of us walking, but my friend Jorun was the only one who was familiar with this particular trail. It was really nice to have her with us. We never had to worry about staying on the right path.

Whenever the trail divided (which it seemed to do a lot!) Jorun would say, "Go to the left" or "Stay to the right" or "This way is easiest." She knew the way, so we were able to enjoy the scenery and the exercise and trust her to guide us.

Our heavenly Father knows that you and I need a guide also, someone to remain with us and help us. In planning redemption through Christ, God knew that we would need someone to stay with us and always be available to us, so He promised, "I will put my Spirit in you and you will live." (Ezekiel 37:14)

When we accept Christ we are instantly indwelt by the Holy Spirit of God and He never leaves us! He stays to encourage, comfort, intercede, strengthen and enable. He is a personal guide, someone to "come alongside" and reveal not only the pathway to God, but how to stay on that path.

The Spirit of God within us knows the pathway we should take. God's Word tells us that we have the "very thoughts of Christ" within us (1 Corinthians 2:15 PHILLIPS) and we have "an anointing from the Holy One, and all of you know the truth." (1 John 2:20)

When God asks us to walk on His path, we can be certain that He has provided all we need in order to be able to do so. He does not want the choices we face to be our downfall. He wants them to be a means to come closer in relationship to Him as we learn to be guided by His Spirit within us.

People were created to be directed and energized by the Spirit of God, but we've lived for so long without knowing the flow of His Spirit through us that it takes time to begin to understand and take hold of His help. It takes time for us to be able to trust in "our guide." As our journey to relationship with God begins, often we find our way only through trial and error because we don't know how to listen to this new advisor.

Jorun would not have been much help to us on the trail if we had ignored her instructions or been talking so loudly we didn't hear her. That is often the way we try to walk with God on life's pathway. The loud voices of our own soul (mind, will and emotions) constantly shout out thoughts, feelings, opinions and choices. We are very used to following them.

Some people have a tendency to follow their feelings. Their daily decisions are influenced by the ups and downs of their emotions. Others are driven by their wills, always striving to obtain the goals and desires their own will dictates. For some, their intelligence is the guide they heed. They have learned to place great confidence in their ability to reason and decide for themselves what is the right path. Although God gave us minds with which to think and discriminate, even this must come into submission to the Spirit of God.

Because we are used to listening to our own thoughts, we often can't "hear" the Spirit of God within us. But God is patient. He guides us with a firm hand while we learn to know and listen to the voice of His Spirit. As long as we desire to walk on His path, God continues to direct with whatever means it takes, bringing us back when we make mistakes and using them to mature us.

"Walking in the Spirit," as Paul described it, is the only way God planned for you to walk on His path and it is the only way you can walk in trust. Circumstances, our own emotions and even our own reasoning, will cry loudly, "Go this way! No! This is the right path!" or "Here, over here! This is the road!" It will always be easier, in the face of great difficulties or pressing circumstances which demand a choice, to take the pathway circumstances dictate, to follow after the crying of our own desires or to try and figure them out logically.

Elisha was hiding at Horeb — afraid for his life, depressed and feeling sorry for himself because of his circumstances — when God told him to "go out and stand on the mountain in the presence of the Lord, for the Lord is about to pass by." 1 Kings 19:11 says that a "great and powerful wind tore the mountains apart and shattered the rocks before the Lord, but the Lord was not in the wind. After the wind there was an earthquake, but the Lord was not in the earthquake. After the earthquake came a fire, but the Lord was not in the fire. And after the fire came a gentle whisper." When Elijah heard it, he pulled his cloak over his face and stood at the mouth of the cave. God began to talk to him just as He will talk to you. It is in the gentle whisper of the Spirit that God makes His path known to you and me.

Not by might, nor by power, but by my Spirit says the Lord Almighty.
–Zechariah 4:6

Don't let the screaming of your circumstances, the roaring of your own intellect or the burning of your own desires dictate the paths you should walk. Learn to listen for the gentle whisper of God's voice through His Spirit. God's will is always known by His Spirit, given to each of us to come alongside and reveal the path He sets before us.

Again and again, as we come to the questions and crossroads in our lives, we must be willing to listen to the guide He has provided. We can trust Him to show us the right path to take.

And the Lord shall guide thee continually.

–Isaiah 58:11 (KJV)

Learning to know God's voice and walk with Him on His path takes time, but it can be an exciting adventure. Decision making is a great learning tool and as we call out to God for help, He is very willing to show us His paths and teach us to know His voice. Remember:

1. We must be careful when there are choices to be made not to assume that something is God's will because it makes us feel good or because it is what we've always wanted. We have to remember that the opportunities, circumstances, and people that come our way will not all be put there by God. Every choice must be prayerfully considered with a heart submitted to doing whatever God says.

2. When we are walking through times of hardship that have thrust us into greater dependence on God, we must allow God to take us all the way through that path, letting Him bring about a change in His time. We must be extra careful when we are on a rocky path to keep looking to God for strength to continue on in submission. When we are weary and discouraged, we may begin to look around for another path. Satan will be quick to provide one.

3. Submission to God and His plans is important in every kind of pathway — prosperous or successful times as well as times of struggle. David stayed home from battle as his reign became more comfortable. During his leisure, he "happened" upon Bathsheba.

4. Be careful of shiny red convertibles: those things that appeal

to our flesh by satisfying unmet needs or unfulfilled desires too conveniently, or the bright new things that appear just when we have taken new steps of growth in our spiritual walk. There will always be opportunities and choices that can cause us to stumble or wander off God's pathway. God will guard us from trials we are not ready to handle (…the Lord knows how to deliver the godly out of temptations. 2 Peter 2:9 NKJV) but we will face temptation. It is often during these times that what is really in our hearts is revealed.

5. Every pathway must line up perfectly with His Word. It soon becomes apparent that the paths Satan or our own carnality point out to us will always be a compromise of either the written Word of God or the specific direction of the Holy Spirit.

6. In *In Search of Guidance,* F. B. Meyers teaches about the "three lights" that must line up to give us direction. They are the inner voice, God's Word and circumstances. He writes, "God's impressions within and His word without are always corroborated by His providence around, and we should quietly wait until those three focus into one point."

Godly Paths

When God through His sovereignty brings us into new situations, we should immediately make sure that our natural life submits to the spiritual, obeying the orders of the Spirit of God.

–Oswald Chambers, *My Utmost for His Highest*

Have you bought a red convertible lately? Do you routinely make important life decisions without consulting God? Do you have a tendency to take off on other paths when the one you're on becomes difficult?

How do you make your important decisions? Do you consider God? How do you determine the path you are going to take? Do you lead the way and expect God to follow?

Do you base your decisions on whatever will temporarily bring comfort? Or are you endeavoring to learn "by experience" to know God's voice? Do you take the time to listen for His voice?

I have learned to daily ask for the mind of Christ and ask the Holy Spirit's help in knowing God's will for me that day. Over the years, my own propensity to error as caused me to cry, "God, please help me to know Your voice!"

Study

Read each Scripture below and write what each says God promises to do for us.

Psalm 32:8 ______________________________

Psalm 48:14 ______________________________

Psalm 37:23 ______________________________

Isaiah 58:11 ______________________________

Read Deuteronomy 13:4. What is our responsibility? ____________

____

Read Isaiah 52:12. What is one important principle to remember in decision-making? ______________________________

____

Read Proverbs 20:27 and Psalm 119:105. How does God light our way?

____

____

Read John 10:14. What does Jesus say about His sheep? Is this true of you?

____

____

Memorize

Now unto him that is able to keep you from falling, and to present you faultless before the presence of his glory with exceeding joy, to the only wise God our Saviour, be glory and majesty, dominion and power, both now and for ever. Amen.
Jude 24-25 (KJV)

Prayer of Response

Dear Father, I need to learn how to walk in the Spirit more consistently. Please help me to learn to differentiate between my thoughts and Yours. I know Your voice is gentle and quiet. It is so easy to miss in the clamor of my own thoughts, desires and circumstances. Teach me to know Your voice, so I can follow more closely by Your side. Your path is the only one I want to walk on. Amen.

Reflect

1. Do you have a "red convertible" experience in your past you can share with others?
2. Was there a time when you thought you heard God saying something to you but it turned out not to be? What did you learn from the experience?

Slow Paths

I glanced over the long line of people standing at the cash register, looked down at the item in my hand and then back at the line again. Did I really want this blouse badly enough to wait in that line? I decided to stand in line, but when two minutes passed and no one moved, I decided I didn't need the blouse, put it down and walked out of the store.

I don't like waiting. I don't like waiting for red lights to change. I don't like waiting in line at the grocery store. I don't like waiting for late planes and I don't like doctors who make you sit in the waiting room for hours.

I'm not alone in my lack of patience. Waiting is something with which many of us have problems. Even those who patiently wait for planes, doctors and slow clerks in the supermarket can be reduced to a quivering mass of anxiety when life throws a curve and they want out of the mess quickly.

It's tough. Most of the waiting we do has an end in sight. The light will turn green, the checkout line eventually moves ahead, the plane arrives and the doctor finally sees us. But in some of the circumstances that come our way, waiting is coupled with the uncertainty of how long it could be before our situation changes, or if it ever will. Waiting becomes intolerable.

People have always had a problem with waiting. In most of the situations we face, God's timing will not be fast enough for us:

"God, it's been 15 minutes, what are You waiting for?"

"God, it's been 30 minutes. Can't You see this mess?"

"God, it's been an hour…I can't stand it much longer."

Yet our ability to trust God is often tested by the need to wait for Him in many of life's circumstances.

Remember the children of Israel, who camped at the base of Mt. Sinai while Moses received God's laws? When the days dragged on and Moses didn't come down from the mountain, their fledgling trust in God failed. They demanded that Aaron give them a new god to lead them.

Saul was told to wait for Samuel before going into battle. As the new king of Israel, Saul, along with a force of Israelites, headed for Gilgal to oppose the Philistines who had been harassing the tribes of Israel. Samuel had instructed Saul to wait seven days until he arrived to offer a sacrifice, but the situation became critical. The enemy seemed to be everywhere. Saul's army became frightened and began to scatter. The circumstances were screaming for action, so Saul acted. He offered the sacrifice himself.

Our carnality will always shout the need for action, for change and for movement of any kind when we are waiting for God. Often, our unwillingness to submit to God's timetable makes us jump in with both feet and create all new problems for ourselves. Why does waiting seem to be such a part of our lives as Christians? Over and over the need to wait upon God arises in so many of the situations we face, and we cry out to God, "Why are You taking so long?"

God's timing never seems to be what we want. We often despair at His seeming lack of interest in getting us out of our problems or His slowness in moving us along in the direction we want to go. Yet when we are in difficulties or in a forced waiting time, often God wants to use the circumstances we face to do many things in us and for us. We tend to look to God to help for a while, acknowledging some sin, making a new dedication, learning some new principles — but in a few months, if the circumstances have still not changed, we are climbing the walls wanting God to do something. Anything! Just hurry up!

God's work in us takes more time than we realize. He is doing much more in us than we can comprehend. We're convinced everything can be done quickly. "Just show me what You want to change in me, God, and I'll change it," or "What are You trying to teach me in this, Lord? I'll learn it. Just hurry up!"

But much of what is accomplished by the Spirit of God within us only comes about through a gradual, day by day tearing down of our carnal self and a gradual building up of our spiritual self. Often, being forced to wait is the only thing that brings us to our knees in surrender. It is the only thing that forces us to keep seeking God, thereby allowing Him to deal with us.

The slow passage of time when we are waiting, the unrelenting sameness day after day, the pain that never stops, the situation that never seems to change and the problem that continues to bring heartache all work to bring us directly into confrontation with God. In that encounter we may become more pliable in God's hands. We may become more willing to be changed. In our eagerness to find relief from the pain of our situations, we may become ready to surrender to God's hand in our life. He is able to accomplish many things in us.

It takes time for God to bring us to the place where we are teachable. It takes time to break down that self-centered core that permeates our entire life and direction. It takes time to bring maturity into our lives. It takes time to draw us into a closer relationship, and it takes time to develop an attitude of trust in each of us. So God makes us wait and, while we wait, He chisels and cuts, shapes and molds. He draws our attention away from the desires of our heart so we will place our eyes upon Him. We learn to trust. When we continue to walk in a trial for months and years, we can be assured that God wants to accomplish much more than what may be obvious at first.

During the years of struggling my husband and I endured with our business, God was doing much more than just teaching us to trust Him in spite of the circumstances. He dealt with the sin, self-sufficiency and materialism in our lives and the lives of our children. He developed patience and reliance upon Him. We received understanding and sympathy for others and learned innumerable lessons about prayer and guidance. He strengthened our desire to know His voice and walk in His path while He showed us His perspective and revealed His values and goals for us.

It is hard to wait upon God, yet the problems we face, the dreams we cherish and the hope we continue to grasp all must be brought to the feet of Jesus and placed there as we surrender ourselves to God. Then as we submit to Him and choose to allow God to do whatever He wants in us and in our situations, we must also choose to let Him do it in His time.

Linda's story is a wonderful example.

It was only a month until the wedding. The invitations had been sent, the bridesmaid dresses were bought and ready, there were shower gifts and early wedding presents already stacked throughout the house. But Linda was beginning to feel she should not go through with it.

It wasn't an easy decision. She loved her fiancé, but she had recently become aware that his commitment to God was not the same as hers. She was feeling more sure that this marriage was not God's will for her life.

In the years that followed her decision to cancel the wedding, I'm sure she wondered if she had made the right choice. Her 25th birthday came and went, her 28th, her 30th and her 35th. All the time, her desire for a husband and family never changed.

Linda filled her life with friends, church and work, continuing to serve God and to seek His best in her life. She enjoyed her sister's children, but wondered if she would ever have any of her own. Linda was probably tempted over and over to become impatient with God. She may have questioned God's timing, His plan and even His involvement many times.

But one spring several years ago we sang a beautiful benediction (based on Ecclesiastes 3:11) at Linda's wedding:

"In His time, in His time
He makes all things beautiful
in His time.
Lord, please show me every day,
as You're teaching me Your way,
that You do just what You say
in Your time."

This is trust, the kind of trust that allows Him to bring beauty into our lives in ways we would never dream, in areas we could never imagine. In perfect design and purpose, He will lay His path before us and help us to walk upon it. But it will always be in His time.

Be still before the Lord and wait patiently for him.

–Psalm 37:7

Unanswered Prayers

Maybe you are reading this and you are in God's "waiting room." Right now your heart is crying "when":

When will I find someone to love me?

When will my marriage be better?

When are my children going to come to Christ?

When will I have a baby?

When will I enjoy good health?

When will I get out from under these financial pressures?

When? When? When?

I've been in this waiting room, too. Not just with our business but in other situations as well. I know how difficult it is! I know the disappointment, the hurt and the feeling that God doesn't care. This is one of the hardest "trusting" lessons we face, yet it probably does the most to pry our fingers away from the expectations we have of "other things" we think we need to be happy.

The last part of Psalm 17:15 says, "When I awake, I will be satisfied with your likeness." Unanswered prayers can help us be satisfied with God.

Study

Read Psalm 69. David was in despair. What was a big part of his despair? (v.3) ____________________

Which verse could have a "however" in front of it because of its change in tone?____________________

What desire is coupled with waiting in Isaiah 26:8?

____

Could waiting have brought it about? Is it your desire?

____

Read Romans 5:3-4. Suffering produces ____________________,

which in turn produces ______________________________________.

Read James 1:3-4. What is the finished product of perseverance?

____

Where do we get the ability to persevere? (Galatians 5:22)

____

Memorize

But I trust in you, O Lord; I say, "You are my God." My times are in your hands. Psalm 31:14-15a

Prayer of Response

Dear Father, I need Your help today. I can't seem to get over the hurt that this waiting brings. Help me to turn my eyes to You. Renew a spirit of praise in me today and help me to focus on Your goodness, Your faithfulness, Your lovingkindness and Your mercy. Forgive me for the blame and the anger in my heart toward You and restore me to intimate fellowship with You. Amen.

Reflect

1. Waiting is difficult, but it does bring rewards. Share with a friend about a waiting time in your life. Were you able to wait until God brought about His plans?
2. Have you been receiving the "perfect work" or "maturity" (James 1:4) in your life that waiting is supposed to bring about? If not, do you think a change in attitude might help?
3. Proverbs 13:12 says "Hope deferred makes the heart sick." Has your heart been too sick to receive the good God wants to accomplish in you during your time of waiting? Ask for His help right now in turning away from any bitterness of heart to trust and praise in His goodness.
4. Look up Psalms 31:14-15a and pray them out loud to the Lord.

The Path of Contentment

Even though it was well into the lunch hour when we entered the restaurant, we could see some empty tables. *There shouldn't be a problem getting a seat,* I thought.

My friend Marci and I had already been to one restaurant, only to find it had closed. This was our second choice, but we had been assuring each other that it would be just as good.

The hostess came over and quickly told us that there was no seating in the non-smoking area. I pointed to some empty tables only to have her snappishly inform me that there was a large party coming in and the waitress for that area would be too busy for us. She then looked at us in silence as if to say, "So why don't you leave?"

I looked at Marci. We stood there for a few seconds, trying to decide what to do. Grudgingly, the hostess finally told us that there was an empty area in the smoking section if we'd like to try it.

We agreed because our time was limited. She took us to a table, gave us water and menus and told us someone would be right with us. We decided what we wanted, closed our menus and waited.

And waited.

And waited.

Continuing to glance at my watch, I saw the minutes ticking by. We were in an empty section and the restaurant was laid out so that areas were concealed from each other, but surely someone knew we were there. About the time I decided we had been abandoned, the hostess brought in several groups of people and seated them all around us.

Finally, a waitress appeared, hurried over to the other tables, took their orders and disappeared again before we could get her attention. At about the same time, everyone started lighting cigarettes. I don't know what I expected — we were in the smoking section, but nevertheless, I started to cough loudly, glaring at the smokers and waving my water glass menacingly.

After a few more minutes, feeling thoroughly frustrated, I got up to look for some help. I spotted a table in another area where no one was smoking and a waitress was hovering. I asked if we could move to her area and then went back to get Marci.

We settled in, the waitress came hurrying over to ask what we wanted and I settled back with a relieved sigh.

I quickly gave my order, handing the menu back to the waitress, only to have her apologize and say, "We're out of that."

I grabbed the menu back, scanned it quickly and asked for something else.

"Oh, that shouldn't be on the menu, they don't make that anymore. I'm sorry," she apologized again.

Barely containing my frustration, I ordered soup and half of a chicken salad sandwich on toasted raisin bread.

"We don't use the raisin bread on half orders."

I looked at her in disbelief while Marci, after a glance at my face, quickly said, "Make it a whole order, then, and two bowls of soup. We'll share the sandwich."

The waitress hurried off while I looked over at Marci and said, "Can you believe this?"

A few minutes later, our order arrived. The waitress asked if we needed anything else and then rushed off as we looked down at the sandwich. The chicken salad, what there was of it, lay between two pieces of…well, it looked like charcoal, but I guess it was their version of "toasted" raisin bread.

"Why doesn't this surprise me?" I muttered.

Marci laughed and then offered to pray. We bowed our heads and she blessed the food and our conversation, ending with, "and, Lord, help us to be content in all things!"

I looked up in time to see her grin wickedly before she dodged my kick under the table. Then she cheerfully removed the chicken salad from the charred bread and began to eat.

I hate it when she does that Pollyanna routine on me. There was no reason for her to be so "holy" about it all. Especially since I had been handling everything pretty well, too, considering.

Sure, I had grumbled some, but I hadn't snarled at the hostess, thrown water on the smokers or told the waitress what I thought of the service or the food. I hadn't lost my temper and I hadn't yelled at anyone. Just how much "contentment" did she want anyway?

What did she really expect in those circumstances?

And what, I wonder, does God really expect?

* * *

Getting through lousy lunches may not throw a curve at your contentment level like it does mine. But for each of us there are situations and circumstances that can rob us of joy, threaten our peace and destroy our contentment.

Being contented in all circumstances is not a lesson we learn quickly or easily. My problem with lunch was over in a few hours, but that is not the case in many situations; some circumstances do not end so quickly. Many times the situations in our lives that threaten our contentment are ongoing. Sometimes they continue to escalate in intensity.

Some difficult circumstances drag on for years and years — chronic illness, an unsaved spouse, wayward children, financial difficulties — and in these kinds of situations we will be frustrated, depressed, anxious and angry as the hopelessness or endlessness of our circumstances threatens to overwhelm us again and again. We spend a great deal of time asking God to change our circumstances. Although change may be what God has in mind eventually, contentment in Him may be His goal for us presently. He does want us to learn to say as Paul did, "I have learned the secret of being content in any and every situation." (Philippians 4:12)

Have you learned to be content in God? Has He become "enough" for you to feel content, or do you continue to allow your circumstances to rule your emotions and destroy your contentment? Whenever we cannot find contentment and security in God during a circumstance, we are saying, in effect, that God and our relationship with Him are not enough for us.

When the landscape of our lives suddenly shifts and we find ourselves on unfamiliar, frightening or painful terrain, our initial emotions of fear, uncertainty or sorrow are to be expected. But in any situation that is ongoing, when we have the chance to daily come to God for the contentment He alone can give and yet we still fret and complain, then we are saying to God, "You are not enough for me."

I must have _______________ in order to be content.

I have to have pleasant surroundings.

I have to have money to spend.

I have to feel loved by someone.

I have to feel important and useful because of a job, ministry, position or family.

I have to have good, successful children.

I have to be healthy.

And on and on.

* * *

My favorite example of contentment is a story in 2 Kings about a woman who lived during the time that Elisha was a prophet in Israel. She lived in the town of Shunem. When she noticed that Elisha passed through her town often, she made a point of asking him to stop at her house for a meal. She then urged her husband to make a small room and furnish it for Elisha so that he could stay with them whenever he came that way.

Elisha enjoyed this hospitality and soon wanted to do something in return for the Shunammite woman. One day as Elisha was resting in the room she had prepared for him, he told Gehazi, his servant, to call her. As she stood before Elisha, he asked her what she would like.

"You've been kind to us. What would you like me to do for you? Would you like me to speak to the king for you or the captain of the host?" In other words, "Do you want money, prestige, attention?"

However, she answered, "I dwell among mine own people."

She did not take him up on his offer to change her circumstances. She was saying, in essence, "I am content."

But perhaps her circumstances were already "perfect." Maybe she didn't need any outside help to make her life better because she simply didn't have any needs or unmet desires.

After answering Elisha, the Shunammite woman left the room. Gehazi then mentioned to Elisha that she did not have a child.

The woman's assurance of contentment is much more intriguing in the light of this new information. She lived in a time when childlessness was considered a horrible curse. Her circumstances were far from "perfect," yet she still said that she was content with her life.

What an amazing woman! In the middle of a situation that was called "cursed" by her society, she could say to Elisha, "I don't need anything. I am content."

This woman had learned that contentment does not depend on perfect lives. It depends on focus. It comes from within as we learn to look away from ourselves and our life situations and look to God. The ability to be content, no matter what the circumstances, will belong to those who have learned to take their eyes off themselves and their circumstances and place them on God. The focus of our attention will determine the extent of our contentment.

Gaining contentment in God during difficult days means we have to ruthlessly tear ourselves, our thoughts and our emotions away from the octopus-like circumstances that surround us with their entangling tentacles, and instead focus on God and His goodness. It will mean asking God over and over for help in trusting in spite of the circumstances, because if our desire is to look to God and believe in His goodness and in His control over our lives, God can help us to learn to be content.

Contentment in all circumstances is a state of being that has to come from deep within and permeate our emotions and our reactions to all that life throws our way. It's like a plumb line that may swing around a little bit when pushed, but it always comes back into place in a straight up and down line. The weight at the bottom ensures that it will come back to rest in a perfect vertical line. God within us is the weight on the plumb line of our contentedness. If we have decided that He "is the blessed controller of all things," and if we have decided to "acknowledge

Him" in all things, then we have given Him the necessary weight to always bring us into a perfect alignment of contentment with Him.

We were created to be God-filled and God-directed. As we allow Him to have His rightful place in our lives and as we begin to seek after Him in all things, we are allowing God Himself to fill our lives with His purpose and His meaning. We will find our contentment is in Him.

Looking to God

What is your area of need in the "contentment" realm? Do you, like me, have an ongoing struggle because of a crusader, make-everything-right personality? Or are you facing a deeper need to be content while enduring ongoing disappointment?

Contentment is a byproduct of an intimate relationship with God. When we come to Him in all circumstances, He will extend His grace to walk through the difficult days, His counsel to help us know which steps to take and His assurance that He is in control of our circumstances. We will realize once again that our contentment is in Him.

Study

Hebrews 13:5 tells us to be content with ______________________.

Read Philippians 4:11. In what situations did Paul say he was content?

____

Read Galatians: 5:22-23. Look at the fruits of the Spirit listed. Which ones are needed for contentment? ________________________

____

List the things you do not have that you have been regarding as essential to your happiness. ______________________________

____

____

In light of the above Scriptures, how can you look at those things differently? ______________________________

____

____

Memorize

I am not saying this because I am in need, for I have learned to be content whatever the circumstances.
Philippians 4:11

Prayer of Response

Dear Father, I realize I have been insisting that I must have __________ in order to be content. Please forgive me and help me to realign my thinking. Help me to be content in You and with what You have already given me. Amen.

Reflect

1. Share with a friend the things that rob you of contentment.
2. Pray for one another that God would enable each of you to receive contentment in those areas through an outpouring of Christ's nature in you.

Dark Paths

When I was a child, my parents went camping with several other couples every year, riding horses into the Sierra Mountains.

They had to pack whatever they needed — tents, sleeping bags, clothes and food — in large barrels. Then on horses and mules they would ride along narrow mountain trails until they came to a beautiful area by a stream. There they camped year after year. They cooked over a campfire, hunted and fished, hiked and relaxed. The guide would leave them with a few horses, coming back 10 days later to take them back to "civilization."

The first day in camp, careful instructions were given regarding landmarks and trails so everyone knew how to get back to the campsite. Because they camped in the same area every year, they had begun to depend on a certain landmark to guide them. It was a huge rock formation settled into the top of a mountain peak. No matter where they went or how far away they hiked or hunted, they could always see that rock and find their direction.

The ladies also carried rifles. Although none of them ever killed anything, they faithfully "hunted." My mother started out one morning, and after an hour or so, she spotted some deer ahead. They bounded off so she began to follow, walking and climbing, trying to quietly stay on their trail. She continued to see them but never got quite close enough to shoot. She kept following, spurred on by the thought that everyone would be surprised if she actually killed a big deer. Finally, after hours of trailing them, she began to tire and decided to give up and head back to camp.

Turning to look up, she searched the horizon for the rock, but it wasn't there. Puzzled, she kept turning in a circle, staring off in every direction to find her landmark. She still couldn't see it. She was in a good position, high enough up to have a good view in all directions, so she was perplexed by this.

I couldn't have walked that far, she thought. She put her rifle to her eye and searched through the scope, but it didn't bring the landmark into view either. As she contemplated which way to go, she began to feel panic creeping up inside. She did not have a good sense of direction — she found it easy to get turned around in a city — and here she was in the middle of the Sierra Mountains.

Mom started off walking in one direction, then nervously turned back around and headed another way. Totally confused, she spent an hour walking in different directions, trying to find her landmark. The rock still didn't appear.

Really frightened, she sat down and began to cry. Through her tears she cried, "God, please help me. I don't know where I am. I can't find the rock!"

As she sat there trying to regain her confidence, she began to notice the ground she was sitting on. It was sheer granite. As she stared at it, realization dawned. She was on it! She was right on top of the rock for which she had been searching so desperately. Her pursuit of the deer had led her to climb much farther than she had realized. All the time she thought she was lost, she had actually been standing on the landmark.

Her tears turning to laughter, Mom quickly walked around the rock until she saw the formation that pointed her way back to camp. Soon she was confidently on her way.

My mom's experience is a wonderful analogy of what sometimes happens in our lives. Sometimes as troubles surround us, our vision gets blurred, the path becomes dark and we look around and think, *Where am*

I? Are you watching God? I shouldn't be here! This can't be Your will for me!

There seems to be no possible good in the situation. The endlessness of it frightens and depresses us. We struggle with doubts and fears. We're certain we've taken the wrong turn somewhere and gotten off the path. We can't see God working anything out at all and despair grips us.

It's difficult not to be anxious when the path we're walking on seems to fade away into obscurity or we lose sight of our landmark or goal, especially when we are forced to try to find our way through scorched valleys or mountainous terrain. As we try to catch sight of the path again, we often conclude that we took a wrong turn back there somewhere. Somehow we missed it. Why else would we be scrambling through washed-out gullies and climbing huge rocks? How else could we lose sight of a clear path?

We can become very frightened as we contemplate the situation and we often begin to try to find where we could have gone wrong. Spiritual soul-searching and examination are good at times in order to check our own willingness to walk upon God's path. We must always be open to God's searchlight to reveal any sin or willfulness that may have taken us off the road. But when our spiritual check-up yields only the conviction that we desperately want to be on God's path — then it is time to stop fretting and start trusting.

This isn't always easy. When the path is dark before us or the way seems consumed with boulders and washouts, it's not only difficult to keep trusting, it is sometimes hard to keep walking. We instinctively want to worry, to question, and to try to backtrack. We want to trace our steps back to the place where we had some light or the path was easier.

Yet our part is always to keep trusting. Our faith keeps us moving spiritually. God is responsible for the rest. He will help us to get on the right path and to stay on it. He will help us to continue to walk when there's no landmark to reveal the right path, even when there is darkness all around and we see no purpose or direction at all.

A darkened path may involve waiting. But a physical waiting in our lives can still be a spiritual journey. A darkened path may involve continuing to work in a situation or ministry where God has placed us, in spite of a lack of results. And the path can be dark when a storm of harsh circumstances begins to rage around us or when God seems to be silent. With no visible path, it's very easy to succumb to questioning and despair.

But when we choose to trust in God in spite of the dark, we are walking on God's path. When we choose to continue to do His will, even when we can't see the purpose, we are walking on His path. And when we choose to honor Him with a commitment even when He is silent, we are walking on His path.

A darkened way is given to those the Lord is ready to bring into a deeper relationship with Him. It is given to those who God wants to stretch and grow, to mold and mature, into His image. People on these paths are given the choice to keep walking with God even when they don't know where He is leading them; to keep going even when the landmarks are gone and they're not sure where they are.

This is trust, trusting God in spite of everything, and it will bring grace and blessing because God gives a darkened path when He wants us to see only Him.

Let Him who walks in the dark, who has no light, trust in the name of the Lord and rely on His God.

–Isaiah 50:10

At some point, the darkness will drop away and our spiritual eyes will suddenly focus upon the path. We will recognize that God has been guiding us all along. All the time that we thought we were wandering aimlessly around, getting nowhere, God was actually drawing us farther along. All the time we thought the boulders and gullies were slowing us down, they were actually leading us to a higher place. And when we thought we were lost, we were actually standing upon the Rock.

Trust in the Lord forever, for the Lord, Jehovah, is the Rock eternal.

–Isaiah 26:4

Light for the Way

Do you feel you are walking in the dark? Are you experiencing confusion or uncertainty about what God is trying to accomplish in you with the circumstances you are currently facing?

Does God seem distant? Are you having difficulty hearing His voice, even though you are trying desperately to find direction and help?

You may be at a new kind of trusting point with God, one in which His face is hidden for a while. But if He trusts you enough to allow you to walk through this kind of circumstance, then you can be sure He is confident in your ability to walk through this time of darkness.

Study

Read 2 Samuel 22:29. What does God promise to do in darkness?

____

Read Isaiah 58:11. What does God promise to do in barren places?

____

Read Psalm 77:19. What does God promise to do even when we can't see where He is leading? ______________________________

Read Psalm 142:3. When we are discouraged about the path we are on, about what can we be confident? ______________________________

Read 2 Chronicles 32:31. Consider this Scripture. Do you realize what God is doing when He is silent? ______________________________

Memorize

Let Him who walks in the dark, who has no light, trust in the name of the Lord and rely on his God.
Isaiah 50:10

Prayer of Response

Dear Father, I accept whatever path You choose for me. Help me not to be afraid of dark paths or uncertain times but to continue growing in trust through whatever circumstances You allow into my life. Help me to remember in times of darkness that even though I can't see You, You are still with me and still watching over me. Amen.

Reflect

1. Read Proverbs 25:2 and think about its meaning.
2. Have you discovered anything new about what is in your heart during God's silence?

A Perfect Path

"Jerry has a red Corvette!"

My teenage kids could hardly wait to inform me of this new development one day when I picked them up after school.

"He does? I didn't know he was old enough to drive," I answered.

"He just turned 16 and his parents gave him a Corvette!" Jula repeated the information in an awestruck voice.

"A new one? Are you sure it was a Corvette?" I thought perhaps it was an older fixer-upper his father had found at a bargain price that just looked like a Corvette.

"It looks new to me," I heard back.

We all rode along quietly for a moment until I said, "That kind of makes it hard on the rest of you kids, doesn't it? The ones who have to live in the real world."

"Yeah. I'll be lucky to get an old Civic!" Matt said.

Life isn't perfect. Not for my kids, not for me and not for you.

It never will be, even when we are right in the middle of God's will. We live in a world and a society deteriorated by sin. No matter how we try, we will never make it perfect. Even if we somehow stumbled onto a "perfect path," we'd soon mess it up because we are far from perfect people.

When you find your first home and everything falls into place for you to buy it, that does not mean that life in that house will be perfect. The roof might leak, the garbage disposal could break, the water heater might wear out and moths could eat your clothes. Even though you wait and pray and God helps you get a good deal so you can finally purchase the car you've been wanting, that still doesn't mean the car will never break down, your kids won't spill milk all over it or you'll never get a flat tire.

God will never so bless your life that it will be completely free of the stresses and problems of living in this world. Cars break down, roofs leak, kids skin their knees, vacation plans get ruined, we miss appointments and tragedies do happen. Even as we learn to walk in the Spirit and learn to lean upon God for everyday help and guidance, we will never come to the place of no problems or disappointments in our lives.

This is not a sign that God doesn't love you, nor that He isn't taking care of you. It is not a sign that He didn't guide you and it doesn't mean you are on the wrong path. Problems are the consequences that we all suffer from sin in the world.

The "perfect" husband who God brings into your life will probably snore and throw his socks on the floor. The "wonderful" wife God provided for you will burn some dinners, start crying for no apparent reason and expect you to remember your anniversary! The "delightful" children that God gives you may have crooked teeth, bad eyesight, learning problems or strong wills; and at some point they are going to drive you crazy.

We won't have perfect husbands, perfect wives, perfect kids, perfect houses or perfect lives. There will be relationship problems. There will be broken furniture and empty gas tanks. There will be hurtful people, hard bosses, unfair situations and most of us don't get a Corvette when we're 16.

Life is like that. Living in Christ does not mean He will keep us from all sorrow and problems.

In this world you will have trouble. But take heart! I have overcome the world. –John 16:33

As we begin to trust God by exchanging our understanding for His and submitting our lives to Him, we'll find that overcoming the world for us does not mean we won't have any more problems. We overcome the stresses and disappointments we face here on earth when they become the stepping stones to deeper awareness of God, the growth of Christ's life in us and greater anticipation and longing for heaven.

Since the fall of man, Jesus is the only perfection that has entered this world. Only when we are finally united with Him for eternity will our lives be perfect. Because our lives on earth are not perfect, we are never going to be free of situations that test our trust in God. Just about the time everything is going well, just about the time we think we've got "trusting" down to a science, the horizon will change and, suddenly, anxiety is sitting on our shoulders, whispering words of fear, turmoil and distrust.

But that's okay. Our initial reactions to circumstances are not a measure of our abilities to trust God. It's how we deal with them. It's what we do with the emotions that threaten to engulf us. It's what we do with the impatience as time continues to drag on. It's what we do with our faltering hopes and shattered dreams.

In all things, we must come to God.

The attitude and emotions we initially bring with us are not important. It only matters that we trust Him enough to come to Him. When we do, God is able to help us. He will give us the ability to let go of the fear and the anger. He will help us pull our eyes away from the overwhelming circumstances and He will give us grace to keep going.

* * *

When God first began to teach me to trust Him, Chuck had just left a secure management job for one in sales. The potential was much greater, but so was the risk. His paycheck was completely dependent upon his sales. It was the perfect learning opportunity, and God certainly used it.

The commission on his sales each month was divided into the two paychecks he would receive the following month. Month after month, the sales seemed to dry up until the very last minute. A sure sale would fall through, leads would go nowhere and the pressure was on. I hated it. As the month progressed, Chuck would come home discouraged over the lack of sales, and as the end of the month loomed closer and closer, my prayers would get more and more intense. It seemed I could only go so far in trusting before I'd finally blow up at God or sink into a poor-me, mistreated-by-God attitude. Then suddenly people would start calling for equipment, lost sales would be resurrected and everything would be okay.

Then I would feel like a worm for not being able to trust God. "Why do You always push me too far? You don't seem to be satisfied until I completely lose my trust in You. Why do You always wait until I blow it?" I would question God even while apologizing for my lack of faith.

But God wasn't pushing me against the wall to see if I'd lose it. He was trying to teach me important principles in trust. Those days of trying to trust Him, and blowing it more often than not, were a foundation for the more advanced opportunities I would have for trusting in the years ahead. Because I wanted to trust God, that desire kept me coming back to Him. Somewhere along the way I finally figured out that I was not able to keep trusting when things looked bad. That despair over my own inability brought me finally to the life-changing knowledge that in this, just like everything else, I needed God's help.

I learned not to wait until my faith was completely destroyed before coming to God for help in trusting Him. I also learned when things got so bad my emotions were out of control, it was okay; I still just needed to come to Him.

As I asked for His Holy Spirit to flow through me, washing away the emotions of fear and distrust, of discouragement or anger, He would flood me again with fresh awareness of His faithfulness. He would give me renewed faith in His intent to bring good into my life no matter what the circumstances might try to scream at me. At the same time God was giving me grace to keep trusting, and pushing out the perimeters of my faith, He was also doing something else even more important.

As we come to Him over and over in days of trouble and nights of fear, we gradually begin to develop a greater capacity for God Himself. During our involvement with Him in trying to get through the painful times of our lives, we come to know Him much more intimately than before and we find that we want to come to Him more and more — not because He changes our circumstances, but because He changes us.

God has so much to give us, so much love, so much more of Himself. The reason we have to walk through situations that try our faith is to mature us past the place where we are happy with just His blessings or the ministries He gives us, because they are only a small part of our relationship with Him.

As we choose to come to Him during difficult days, exchanging our understanding for His and submitting to His ways, we gradually become aware of the joy and fulfillment that we receive while in His presence. We become dependent upon the peace He alone can impart to our souls and we want to experience His presence more and more. Soon He becomes more important than any change in our circumstances. He becomes of greater value than our deliverance from tough situations. As

God satisfies us with Himself, with His love during our times of prayer and communion with Him, He is creating in us a desire for Him. Then as our capacity for God — our enjoyment of Him — increases, so does our ability to trust Him.

Finally, we realize it isn't the path or the circumstances of our life that matter, it is the walk with God on that path. It is the relationship itself that matters. He is the point: knowing Him, experiencing Him, loving Him and receiving His love.

You see, God knows that He can make you happy. You don't really know it yet, not completely. But God is aware of His own indescribable wonder and the capacity for fulfillment and joy that lies within your relationship with Him. We tend to keep Him at arm's length, loving Him as much as we are able given our limited knowledge of Him, but God wants much more than that from us and He has much more love to give us than we are capable of receiving and enjoying.

We also tend to forget that we were created for a relationship with God. That was His intent when He created people and it was His intent when He created you. His fierce desire and intent to love us and be known by us will not rest until He has begun to make us aware of Him. His love means He will be as gentle and loving as we allow Him to be in His pursuit of an intimate relationship with us, but a pursuit it is.

He wants to bring you into ever-increasing intimacy with Him. He wants His love for you to be known by you. Nothing else will bring you joy. Even though we may think that only good circumstances are the way we will be happy, God knows better. We were created for a relationship with Him. True happiness will always lie within the framework of an intimate relationship with God.

A Mighty Love

Do you believe that God loves you? Do you understand yet how vast His love is? Do you realize that when you begin to comprehend His love and receive it more fully it will overshadow everything else?

His love for you is "beyond measure." It surrounds you day by day, moment by moment, covering you, protecting you, guiding you, drawing you to Him; it cannot be stopped. It is continually operating, always wanting to bring good to you. Even those things that come your way that are hurtful and seem so awful are filtered through His love. They never touch you without God knowing that He can use them to bring good into your life.

We see as children. We do not grasp God's love for us. We cannot know it fully in this lifetime. However, God wants us to know His love. He wants us to walk in assurance of it so that His love and care are the foundations of our lives, changing our perceptions of life and its events, covering them with new "understanding" that, though we may experience hurtful things and grief may come our way, His love is bigger than every circumstance. God's love for you is mighty!

Study

Meditate today on the Scriptures at the top of the next page that tell of God's love for you. Underline them in your Bible. You may want to copy them onto cards and put them where you can see them during the day. Read one or two every day. If you are having difficulty grasping God's love for you, try personalizing each Scripture. Read it aloud, realizing God is saying it to you.

Jeremiah 31:3
Zephaniah 3:17
Jeremiah 29:11
Isaiah 49:15-16
Ephesians 2:4-7
1 John 3:1-2
Song of Songs 1:15
Isaiah 43:1-4
Psalms 139:17-18
John 15:9
Romans 5:8
1 John 4:16,19

There is no fear in love. But perfect love casts out fear

Memorize

The Lord appeared to us in the past, saying, "I have loved you with an everlasting love; I have drawn you with loving-kindness."
Jeremiah 31:3

Prayer of Response

Dear Father, help me to stop expecting a perfect life and instead begin to focus on knowing You better. Help me to begin to see the upheavals and problems as opportunities to appreciate all You are, as reminders that only You are perfect and that Your love for me is perfect and without limit. I do want to begin to grow in the knowledge of Your love for me and to learn to love You more. Help me with this process. I know I have failed to spend time in the pursuit of You, just You. Help me to begin to make that my priority. Amen.

Reflect

Think about your successes or difficulties in knowing God's love for you.

The Path of Deliverance

Darlene Keibler Rose, an American missionary, spent four years in a Japanese concentration camp in New Guinea during World War II. She endured unimaginable deprivation and cruelty at the hands of her captors. While there, she learned of her husband's death in another camp.

Just when it would seem her circumstances couldn't get any worse, she was accused of treason and taken from the camp to a prison to be interrogated. There she was put in a filthy, cold, dark cell, and forced to endure endless interrogations. She suffered terribly from dysentery and the horrible, endless torment of mosquitoes and vermin. In the middle of her nightmarish existence it was hard for her to imagine God was there.

One day she heard voices in the courtyard. Jumping to grab the bars that covered the small window high in her bleak prison cell, she pulled herself up and looked outside. There she saw a group of female prisoners who were being allowed to walk around outside. As she watched, the actions of one woman caught her attention. Every time the sentry on duty turned his back, the woman inched over toward a fence covered with vines.

As Darlene watched the woman she assumed she was making contact with someone outside. Soon she saw a hand shoot through the tangle of vines. It had a big bunch of bananas. Quickly the woman grabbed them, slipped them into the folds of her sarong, and then, nonchalantly, she strolled back to join the other women.

Nobody had seen it but Darlene. As she dropped to the floor, exhausted from her efforts, she began to shake. And, as her mind replayed what she had seen, she began to crave bananas. Everything in her wanted one. She could see them. She could smell them.

She finally got down on her knees and said, "Lord, I'm not asking you for a whole bunch like that woman has. I just want one banana." She pleaded, "Lord, just one banana."

Then she began to rationalize: how could God possibly get a banana to me through these prison walls? I would never ask the guard. If he helped me and was discovered, it would mean reprisal. As she thought through her contacts, she realized there was more of a chance that the moon would fall from the sky than her getting a banana from anyone.

So she bowed her head again and prayed, "Lord, there's no one here who could get a banana to me. There's no way for You to do it. Please don't think I'm not thankful for the rice porridge. It's just, well, those bananas looked so delicious."

The next day the prison was visited by Japanese officers. This was a dreaded event because the prisoners were inspected, ridiculed, scorned and insulted. They were forced to bow and were struck if they failed to do so properly.

As Darlene heard footsteps coming toward her cell, she dragged herself to her feet, getting ready to bow. As the cell door opened, she was delighted to see Mr. Yamaji, the commander from the concentration camp where she had been before she was sent to prison. He was kind. It was like seeing an old friend. As he looked at her emaciated state, tears filled his eyes and he quickly turned and walked out into the courtyard to talk with the officers who conducted her interrogations.

Soon he came back and asked if she had any messages for friends back at the camp. When he left she heard him talking to her guard. In a few moments the guard came toward her room. He opened the door, walked in and with a sweeping gesture threw a huge bunch of bananas at her feet. "They're yours," he said, "from Mr. Yamaji."

Darlene sat in stunned silence and counted them. There were 92 bananas! Falling to the ground, she wept in shame. "Lord, forgive me. I'm so ashamed. I couldn't trust You enough to get even one banana for me and just look at them. There are almost a hundred."

In the quiet of the shadowed cell, He answered back within her heart, "That's what I delight to do — exceedingly abundantly above anything you ask or think."

In reading Darlene's account of her years in prison and the many things she suffered, it would be easy to think, "God, if you could give her bananas, why couldn't you just deliver her from the whole thing? Why did she have to endure all that?"

But as we have already established, God does not deliver us from all the evil that will come our way. There will be some painful circumstances we will have to walk through. Some, like Darlene, seem called to walk through unbelievable hardships. But in the middle of her trial, God did not forget about her. He was not looking the other way. He was there with her, caring for her and allowing only so much.

He didn't immediately zap her out of this fiery trial, but he walked with her through it until her total deliverance came. The Japanese were defeated and Darlene was able to go home. There she married again, had children and lived a full life.

While she was in a Japanese prison, however, she didn't know her future. All she knew was hardship, loneliness and fear. But God had not forgotten about her. He was there with her.

And God has not forgotten you. He is with you day by day, moment by moment, no matter what kinds of trials you may be facing. The trials will not go on forever. Deliverance will come.

There is a portion of Scripture in Isaiah 28 about grain needing to be ground for bread that says in part, "One does not go on threshing it forever. Though he drives the wheels of his threshing cart over it, his horses do not grind it." This is a wonderful promise to us that although God allows adversity into our lives, He does not allow it to go on continuously. We can hope and trust in His willingness to save, to help and to deliver.

When we are in the midst of a trial it is easy to get caught up in the negative. Satan, the deceiver, helps us with that. He whispers in our ear. For whatever miracle you are asking or deliverance you are awaiting he says to you, "God doesn't usually do that for people."

He points out the people who did die.

He points out the people who did go bankrupt.

He reminds you of those still living in pain.

He reminds you of marriages that did not make it.

On and on the deluge of negative, false information can come into our minds and hearts, undermining our faith and trust in God. It can be a constant battle to put the truth back into it. God does redeem. God does deliver. God does heal. God does restore lives. The stories abound of what He does. Each of us has a story to tell of God's help, of His intervention and of His redemption of our lives.

We can't know the whole story behind any seeming failure of God to intervene. We don't know what God is doing in other's lives. But gradually in our own lives, if we keep walking with God, we begin to have our own histories of God's intervention and help. We begin to see the reason why a prayer was or was not answered in the way it was.

God directing our path is a great promise to us. We have a tendency to focus on the negative, on the trials and the answers to prayer we don't receive, yet we are constantly within the circle of God's love and grace. We are never outside of His care. God's love for you surrounds you each day. His goodness is extended to you day by day, every moment of every day. Learning to trust God means that we believe in His goodness to us. That belief keeps our lives from becoming blown off course when the waves of hurtful circumstances crash against us.

Believing that God will bring good from every circumstance means we are assured that good will follow any evil which might touch us. Even though life will never be perfect, God is and God's perfection — His unchangeableness — means we can believe in what He says in His word. His love surrounds us, He is always taking care of us and He will never allow anything to touch us from which He cannot bring good. That means there is always hope! If we are living submitted to God's will, we can believe that He will take care of us and bring good into our lives.

It is difficult to know how to write about hope because I know that there is not always a happy ending to every circumstance. Happy endings are not always possible because of the complexity of people's lives, other's choices and varying circumstances that intertwine every situation. However, we can trust that God's goodness is always operating. He will do what is best for all.

Because He is a great and mighty God, He can do abundantly above all we could ask or think. There are many times He wants to do just that. Usually our desired solution leaves too much undone. He has much greater, more complex plans for us.

We must also never be guilty of limiting God's goodness and

ability to do great and mighty things for us and through us because we have learned the lessons of submitting in grace to whatever comes our way. As we submit to God in our circumstances, we should never begin to revel in the acceptance of difficult circumstances and become stuck there, thinking that is the epitome of Christian virtue. God is too multifaceted for us to capture Him in one kind of response to life's situations. He wants to show His power in and through us as He enables us to accept tough situations and empowers us to overcome and trust Him in spite of the unhappy ending. But He also wants to show His power and ability to deliver, to save, to miraculously heal, to restore a hopelessly dead marriage to life again, to rescue you when you are on the brink of bankruptcy, to save that rebellious teenager and to do abundantly above what we could ask or think.

God does have miracles for us. He did come "that we might have life and life more abundantly." Even though abundant life is all about intimacy with God and trust in Him, because God is a great and mighty God, there is more to it than just that. He wants to show you His power to do mighty things. He wants to delight you with good things, and He wants to reward you for your obedience as His goodness and mercy follows you all the days of your life.

Believing in His Power

God wants you to believe in His willingness and His intent to do good for you. Are you having a problem believing that? Have you become so focused on the problem at hand that you forget all God is, all He has done and all He can do?

Sorrows will come our way, but He intends to overshadow them with His love and care and He intends to redeem them. He always intends to do good to us. He intends to bless and provide for us and He intends to redeem our lives from destruction.

In times of adversity, we must learn to look for and expect to see God still working in our lives; covering, helping, giving grace and intervening in many ways even when He doesn't immediately deliver us from our fiery trials. God never forsakes us. When He allows a trial to continue we know He intends to use it for our good and His glory.

But while God is using your problem to bring good to you, He wants you to believe in His willingness and power to do great things in you and for you. He does heal marriages. He does enable us to overcome sin. He does bless financially. He does make dreams come true. He delights in doing good things for His children.

Study

What does the writer of Lamentations say he recalls in 3:19-24? Also read verses 31-33. ______________________________

____

____

____

Read Daniel 6:27. What did King Darius say about God after Daniel was delivered from the lion's den? ______________________________

What are we promised in:

Psalm 145:14 and 19? ______________________________

____

____

Deuteronomy 33:27? ______________________________

____

____

Galatians 1:4? ______________________________

____

____

Colossians 1:13 ______________________________

____

____

Read Zechariah 9:12. What are people who wait for deliverance called?

____

What are they promised? ______________________________

The preceding were Scriptures that tell of deliverance. Next read all of 2 Corinthians, chapter 4. Underline the Scriptures that talk about trials. Especially note verses 8 and 17.

In verse 18, Paul says to fix our eyes not on what is seen, but on what is unseen. In light of what you have been learning in this book, to what do you think "unseen" refers? ______________________________

Memorize

Who shall separate us from the love of Christ? Shall trouble or hardship or persecution or famine or nakedness or danger or sword? No, in all these things we are more than conquerors through him who loved us. Romans 8:35 & 37

Prayer of Reflection

Dear Father, in my quest to persevere with steadfast faith, help me not to limit Your desire and ability to deliver me from fiery trials. As You increase my persevering faith, I ask You to also give me faith to receive the many good things You desire to do for me. I believe You still perform miracles and I want to believe in You for all You are and all You do! I ask You to give me the gift of faith. Amen.

Reflect

1. What distress are you suffering right now?
2. What famine are you experiencing (what are you doing without)?
3. What persecution are you experiencing?
4. Share a story with a friend about deliverance or waiting for deliverance. Share the promise God gave you that helped you (or is helping you) to trust while waiting for His deliverance.

The Path of Trust

I was so glad I had made a chocolate cake earlier that Saturday. The phone rang and I heard my husband answer it. After a few minutes of quiet talk, he came in to the room where I was and told me the house we were renting had been sold. He quickly related that we had to move in two months, then took me in his arms to reassure me before heading outside to pull weeds — his way of dealing with stress.

I headed for the kitchen, cut a large piece of chocolate cake and poured myself a glass of milk. Then I walked upstairs to our bedroom, curled up on my bed, pulled the comforter up over me, and slowly savored the chocolate cake — my way of dealing with stress.

Gloomily, I contemplated our options. None of them looked promising. We had sold our home nearly a year and a half prior to put the equity into our business. Our small company had slowly been pulling ahead after a disastrous couple of years, but it just needed more capital. We felt our equity would be better invested in the business than in our house, so after months of praying, we cautiously proceeded. When our house sold quickly for the amount we wanted, we were encouraged that we were on the right track.

But even while everything worked out for the sale, it was hard to give up my house. We had lived there for nine years and it was familiar, comfortable and full of memories. It had been our physical refuge through some tough years with our business. It had been the place where our son and daughter had progressed from tricycles and skates to 10-speeds, telephones and high school. It had their growth recorded in notches on the door frame in the kitchen. Their worn-out swing set, abandoned for several years now, was still keeping a lonely guard over the play area in the backyard. That house was home, and I struggled with thoughts of insecurity and feelings of being uprooted.

After we began to look at rentals, my emotions plummeted even further. We live in an area where housing costs are among the highest in the nation. I didn't relish leaving my comfortable house for what we found available to rent.

However, God was gracious and to my delighted surprise, a rental fell across our path that was just beautiful. It was larger and newer than the house we had just sold and for some "reason" the owners were offering it at a ridiculously low rent. We "happened" to be the first to see it and quickly signed a year's lease.

We moved in and soon became accustomed to the space and the physical beauty of the area. All of the homes in the area were on one or two-acre parcels, and there was a park right next to us. My feelings of insecurity over not owning my own home quickly vanished as I enjoyed this unexpected gift from the Lord. I knew it was temporary, but secretly I hoped that something would happen…the business that was slowly pulling away from near-bankruptcy would begin to prosper quickly or the house we were in or another in the area would be for sale, and maybe, just maybe, we would be able to buy and stay.

But this day, that hope had been snuffed out. The house had sold before it was even on the market, at a price we couldn't have afforded anyway. I ate another bite of chocolate cake, took a sip of milk and began to think about what lay ahead: moving! Bad enough by itself, but we also faced the question of where. It was hard to give up another house that had become "home" to us. Now we would either have to move to another rental for six months and then move again when we bought a house (we had to purchase again within two years after selling or pay capital gains taxes on the profit) or try to find a house to buy before we had to move. Two months wasn't much time!

Behind these options was the knowledge that most rentals required a year's lease and that the market in our area had continued to skyrocket after we sold our house. New houses were even more unaffordable than before. At this time, it would be very difficult to pull enough money out of the business for a down payment. Our options were really very limited.

I finished my cake and thought about going downstairs for another piece, but then I remembered how much jogging I would have to do in order to compensate for it. So I propped myself back up in bed and turned my questioning to God. "What are we going to do? What are You going to do? What's ahead?" As I began to "deal" with God, struggling with the questions and fears, I realized that in this, too, I would have to trust Him. Quietly, I reaffirmed my faith in His goodness and ability to take care of all my needs.

God's grace immediately enveloped me as it always does when we seek Him in times of distress and, suddenly, I just didn't care. What we would do and where we would live ceased to matter.

Then I realized that God, in His infinite love and care, had already been preparing me for this. The preceding months had been filled with day after day of closeness as He had filled me with an ever-increasing sense of Himself. I had just finished an in-depth study of Song of Solomon and had become even more aware of His great love for me. As I spent time with Him in prayer He daily saturated me with joy in His presence. He constantly reinforced the knowledge that my relationship with Him was all that really mattered. During those times of intimacy, He had placed a giant hook in my heart that continually drew me to Him so that my desire was for Him and Him alone.

Now, as the house we lived in was snatched away, I was awesomely aware that it didn't matter because God was, and would always be, home. Home makes us think of many things — security and comfort, a place where we can be ourselves, a place where our loved ones are, a place where we feel loved and protected — but for all of us who call God "Father," home should eventually bring forth the image of Him.

At some point in our relationships with God, if we allow Him full access into our lives and continue coming to Him even in times of difficulty, He becomes the foundation of our life in such a way that our well-being has nothing whatsoever to do with our physical place, or our circumstances. It has nothing to do with the ups and downs of life, or the kinds of environments we live in. Our security is no longer in a place, a job or in another person. It is in God and God alone.

This transformation in thinking doesn't happen overnight, and it won't happen without experiencing upheaval and turmoil. But somehow, if we will continue to come to God — spending time with Him, talking to Him and learning about Him, if we begin to make Him a part of all of our lives — God will become the place to which we always return.

When He does, we will begin to feel the emptiness of life without Him. We will get so used to His presence and the deep joy and contentment He alone can give that more and more we will be seekers of God. His hook will be planted deep in our hearts, and we will desire Him more than anything else.

If we have allowed the circumstances of our lives to draw us to God, and if we have sought Him out in times of sorrow, discouragement and need, then at some point the grace and help He gives during those times will become secondary to the joy and fulfillment we sense when we are in His presence. We will begin to desire God — not for His help, not for His saving grace, not for His delivering power and not even for His peace and comfort — but simply for Himself.

God's presence becomes the fulfillment of what we were created to enjoy, giving us a sense of security and love, of belonging and of homecoming.

Then God becomes our "familiar place." God becomes our security and our retreat from the hectic world. God Himself is the place where we are accepted and loved. He is our place of rest. Our security is in Him, for He is our home.

Lord, you have been our dwelling place throughout all generations.

–Psalm 90:1

* * *

The path to trust in God is long and varied: sometimes steep and difficult, sometimes bright and easy, sometimes winding and confusing, sometimes breathtakingly exciting and sometimes slow and dark.

It involves many kinds of circumstances:

- Receiving help right when you need it.
- Not getting the thing you "absolutely must have" in order to be happy and then seeing how good it was that God didn't allow it.
- His coming through at the last minute.
- His not coming through at the last minute.
- Waiting and waiting and waiting so long that despair sets in and you finally release that desire because God's presence is more valuable than the object of your endless prayers.
- Wonderful, miraculous answers to prayer.
- Coming to know God's love because pain and unanswered

prayers have caused you to open yourself more fully to Him.

- A complex and meandering path, but all along the pathway God is beside you, guiding, teaching, helping and even carrying you at times as you progress along the pathway to trust and intimate fellowship with Him.

Trust is the bond that forges your relationship with God. It will enable you to know and love Him in ever increasing intimacy. It will bring you joy and peace, and it will allow God to work mightily in you and on your behalf. Trust and faith in God, that He is who He says, and that He will do what He has promised in His Word, begins when we accept Christ. But that is only the initial "step." Again and again we will have to make the choice: will I trust God?

In the times of questioning, our faith in Him is a choice: a choice to believe in His goodness and love to us and a choice to dwell on the many blessings we do have, instead of wallowing in our lists of unanswered prayers, a choice to rest in Him, realizing it is His responsibility to do for us what is best and to show us whatever we need to learn and that our responsibility is to trust and obey.

We have to choose to trust Him. We have to choose to obey Him. We have to choose to give thanks in all things. We have to choose to walk on the path He puts before us.

* * *

You must be willing to come to the edge and look away from your circumstances, your desires and dreams, and your problems and lack of understanding and decide that you will trust God with all your heart. Then as you begin to look to Him in trust, you will begin to exchange your understanding for His and see as He sees. As you "throw" yourself into His arms by submitting to Him in all, you'll find He will catch you every time. He'll always hold onto you and He'll always bring good from your circumstances.

As you journey through life you'll find the path on which you walk to be just the right path for you — a path of trust.

You have made known to me the path of life; You will fill me with joy in your presence.

– Psalm 16:11

It is up to us now to leap off the edge of our circumstances into His waiting arms, and learn to trust God.

Surely this is our God; we trusted in him, and he saved us. This is the Lord, we trusted in Him; let us rejoice and be glad in His salvation.

– Isaiah 25:9

Recommended Reading

The Christian's Secret of a Happy Life
Hannah Whitall Smith

Disappointment with God: Three Questions No One Asks Aloud
Philip Yancey

Finding God: Learning to Hear God's Voice
Dr. Larry Crabb

He Speaks Softly
Bob Benson

The Holiness of God
R.C. Sproul, Jr.

In Search of Guidance
F. B. Meyers

Knowing God
J. I. Packer

My Utmost for His Highest
Oswald Chambers

Predestination and Free Will
edited by David Basinger and Randall Basinger

Psalm 23; The Song of a Passionate Heart: Hope and Rest from the Shepherd
David Roper

Trusting God: Even When Life Hurts
Jerry Bridges

Where Is God When It Hurts?
Philip Yancey

Yet Will I Trust Him
Peg Rankin